Love & Feathers

I have always loved all animals, but birds have become my heart. And that is why I like your book so much. You touch the bird in me.
—**Ellen Cook**, DVM

Love & Feathers is filled with compelling stories about how Shannon's parrot helps her to see aspects of her life from a different view, which fuels her self-growth. It serves as an incredible reminder that many of life's most powerful lessons can be found in the simplest of places.
—**Amy Morin**, LCSW, author of *13 Things Mentally Strong People Don't Do*

A refreshingly unique and beautiful love story, *Love & Feathers* is a laugh-out-loud page-turner. Even if you aren't enthusiastic about birds, you will be about this book!
—**Jenni Schaefer,** Author of *Almost Anorexic*; *Goodbye Ed, Hello Me;* and *Life Without Ed*

I started to read your book—I had no idea what to expect…. It's delightful. I'm not really a bird person, but find myself sucked in. I really like that it's both this personal conversation and really factual, instructional. It made me think about how a loving pet companion might plug up some of the holes in my life.
—**Marcelyn McNeil**, artist and animal lover

Love & Feathers is a joyful journey filled with compassion and wisdom. Shannon shares how a pet, Pearl (who happens to be an avian), can teach us the skills we need to overcome adversity and live our lives to the fullest. Life with Pearl is full of humor, insight and inspiration. A must read for all pet lovers!
—**Maisen Mosley**, parront to **Pongo** (green cheek conure), **Purdy** (Quaker parrot), and three canine "kids"

Dear Shannon, not only is Pearl beautiful, but he is great at teaching others lessons in recovery and acceptance!
—Love, **Megan** (featherless being) & **Dermott** (parrot)

I have followed the exploits of Pearl for some time now, watching with well-deserved admiration as he trains his human Shannon in the ways of cockatiel service. It's all here, from how to feed a cockatiel to those all-important veterinarian visits, all while projecting a semblance of sanity.
—**Marguerite Floyd**, author of *Cockatiel Lessons* and *The Parrot Reckonings*

I 'flew' through *Love & Feathers*—I loved it! Thank you, Shannon and Pearl, for sharing lessons on what really matters in life—love, and living in the moment. For evermore, when I see a parrot, or indeed any bird (or human), I will look beyond the feathers and seek to connect with the love within.
—**June Alexander**, grandmother, mum to two kitties, author of *Hope at Every Age – Developing an Appetite for Recovery* and *A Girl Called Tim*

Love and Feathers is a delightful account of love in its most pure and literal form. It is a story about finding your destiny just when you least expect it. With flawless and comical prose, Shannon allows her readers to see how life can be deeply enriched when you can love someone and be loved in return. Pearl and Shannon are soulmates who share six wondrous things: trust, surrender, sufficiency, peace and endless potential. I adored this book.

—**Emi Berger**, DVM

Love & Feathers took me on a heart-warming journey into the intricacies of avian-human companionship. I was especially intrigued with how Pearl's life was shown to be an example of how we could also enjoy our own life. Those who truly treasure their avian family members will surely grin, giggle and even sigh as they relate to the antics of Pearl. Trust me, you will relate.
—**Sherri Inskeep Lewis**, Past President of the National Cockatiel Society and owner of Tame Tiels Aviary

Near the end of *Love & Feathers*, Shannon writes, "If I want to have a relationship with God, I must seek first and only this: a relationship with love." I cannot possibly find a better way to describe this book. Buy two copies; you are going to want to give it to someone immediately.
—**Thom Rutledge**, author of The *Power of Self-Forgiveness* and *Embracing Fear*

Love & Feathers

what a palm-sized parrot has taught me about life, love, and healthy self-esteem

Shannon Cutts
with Pearl

Copyright © 2015 by Shannon Cutts.

ISBN: 978-1-63490-796-5

Library of Congress Cataloguing in Publication Data
Cutts, Shannon.
Love & Feathers: what a palm-sized parrot has taught me about life,
    love, and healthy self-esteem / Shannon Cutts—1st ed.
p. cm.
1. Pets. 2. Birds. 3. Essays & Narratives.
2015913842

Published by Waffles = Love Press, Houston, Texas, U.S.A.
2015

Printed on acid-free paper.

www.LoveAndFeathers.com

Table of Contents

A Note from the Author

I am not now and will never be an expert on parrot care. In our relationship, Pearl is clearly the teacher and I the willing and eager student.

As such, this book is not meant to suggest that the way I care for my parrot is the way you should care for your parrot. There are all manner of approaches to parrot diet, wellness, enrichment, and other essentials, and each has something worth exploring.

Rather, my goal in writing *Love & Feathers* is simply to offer you a glimpse into the heart of a parront (parrot + parent) who loves her parrot to infinity and beyond—and is lucky enough to receive every bit of that love and more in return.

<u>Part One</u>

Introduction to Love & Feathers

Our Story

I see feeeeeeeeet. And a cute cockatiel beeeeeeeeeeeeak…

I wait. One Mississippi, two Mississippi, three…I can just make out the tip of a diminutive curved grey beak slowly descending from behind the bathroom vanity mirror. Pearl and I are playing "Now You See Me" and Pearl is in charge.

As usual.

When I first met Pearl, I was still mourning the loss of my first cockatiel, a yellow and white bird named Jacob. Jacob was only three years old when he died of congenital kidney failure. His death is still one of the most painful memories of my life. I did not—I repeat NOT—want another cockatiel after Jacob passed.

But my parents knew how much I love birds, and they staunchly believed that a new avian companion could heal me in a way that even time likely would not. Attempting to broach the subject with me was like suggesting I consider enrolling in advanced math classes or taking up soccer—I simply wouldn't hear of it. So unbeknownst to me, they took matters into their own hands, donned their trench coats and dark sunglasses, and started sleuthing for cockatiel babies at nearby pet stores.

One day I was at work as usual when I got an urgent call from my mom. She insisted I had to meet them at a nearby PetSmart during my lunch hour that very day. I as vigorously insisted I didn't want to go. But as moms go, mine can be quite persistent, so at noon on the dot I dutifully pulled into the parking lot. I walked inside and saw both of my folks bending over a large, open-air cage in the center of the store. The cage held at least a dozen exceptionally cute cockatiel babies. The closer I got to the cage, the more reluctant I felt. I wasn't ready. My mom was too pushy. How could she? She should realize I couldn't stand to lose another bird, especially so soon after Jacob's death. As I watched the energetic yellow and white fledglings climbing all over each other to compete for treats and attention, I almost turned on my heel and walked back out the front door.

But then I saw him.

He was huddled in a tiny ball, clearly trying to make himself as invisible as possible. He was a very small grey cockatiel, the obvious runt of the litter, his eyes droopy with fatigue and his downy chest feathers still matted with baby bird formula. He saw me at about the same moment I saw him, and we moved towards each other instinctively.

As I gently lifted him up in my hand—he was so tiny he barely filled my palm—I saw he was missing claws from each foot. The bird department manager softly informed me that this baby's left wing was badly damaged as well and he would probably never fly. The staff suspected his siblings were to blame. I observed how the older, stronger birds totally ignored him unless he happened to get in their way. If this happened they barreled right over him as if he wasn't even there.

Different species aside, I knew EXACTLY how he felt—the runt of the litter, the ugly duckling, the one who looked and felt so different, the one who, try as he might, just didn't fit in.

I looked at him and whispered softly, "You are love with wings, aren't you?" The baby pivoted his tiny grey head, huge round black eyes gazing up into mine. He started to try to climb up my arm but his weak and mostly clawless toes wouldn't oblige. I scooped him up onto my shoulder and he promptly burrowed into my hair, clinging with his soft baby beak to a few wayward strands for balance. We walked around the store like this together until the manager got worried, assumed he had been stolen, and mounted a full-scale search (which, predictably, culminated in my general direction). Determined to keep him, I named him "Pearl."* I then reluctantly handed him back to the bird manager, who said he had not been weaned yet and could not possibly leave the store until he could eat seed like his older brothers and sisters.

"We'll see about that," I muttered rather too violently to myself under my breath as I walked away.

My mom was firmly set against me taking Pearl home. I get my love of animals honestly, and she, too, was still mourning Jacob. Mom wanted me to select one of the older and stronger yellow and white cockatiels instead. I conceded her point and returned to the store the very next day. I picked out a strong yellow male cockatiel and let him sit on my shoulder for a while. He was sweet, but where I had felt a sudden flood of maternal love when I first held his baby brother, I didn't feel much of anything this time. Telling myself it was probably just due to mourning, I went ahead and put the yellow bird on hold. I promised to return the following day at lunch to select a cage and accessories so I could take him home.

Then something very odd happened. Later that night, the scratches on my shoulder from where the strong yellow bird had gripped my bare skin with his eight perfect sharp claws became red and inflamed. Itchy and irritable, I stayed awake all night long. I used the time to try to think of a name for him, but by morning I was still drawing a blank. I returned to the pet store that day at lunch to complete my purchase, hoping his name would come to me once I saw him again. As my folks watched approvingly, I bundled the big yellow baby up in his new cage, complete with food and water bowls, new perches and toys, giant bags of fresh seed, crunchy millet, and assorted deluxe avian accessories. I was standing in line at the cash register, and as I watched cage and bird roll gently down the conveyor belt towards the cashier, from deep within a voice simply said, "I can't."

It was audible. I heard it, my parents heard it, and the cashier heard it. She paused mid-sale and looked at me. I lifted the cage with its big, bold, feathery yellow occupant off the conveyor, walked back to the bird department, and told the manager I had chosen Pearl instead. With a determined look in my eye, I informed her I would feed Pearl the baby bird formula myself until he was fully weaned.

The manager nodded and confided quietly, "If you hadn't taken him I was going to take him home myself." Then she gently lifted little Pearl out of the open-air cage and placed him into my cupped hands.

Love and Feathers is our story.

* *The bird department manager initially informed me Pearl was a female bird. Read on to learn just how wrong she was.*

Yes, My Girl Bird is a Guy Bird

You might be wondering how this fact managed to escape my attention for 11 straight years. A valid question.

When I recently told one of my friends, "Hey, guess what—Pearl is a boy!" she asked me, "How come you didn't know that before? Don't birds have girl and boy parts?"

The answer is "yes" of course; however, the parts are inconveniently located on the inside of the bird. Surgery can find them, but I pity the surgeon who tries to slip past me, scalpel in hand, in an attempt to solve the mystery. Feather or blood DNA testing can also tell, but these tests cost a whopping $25 each and I am a writer after all. Plus, last year my mom bought us a membership to the National Cockatiel Society and those people took one look at Pearl and told me she is a he. Since they breed cockatiels professionally, they probably know what they are talking about.

In fact, according to the good folks at the NCS, repetitive whistling, obsession with shiny objects, vent rubbing (cage bars, remote controls, and apparently pretty much anything else will substitute when a ladybird isn't available) and most tellingly those super-white cheek patches all scream "male bird." Who knew? Clearly not me.

So here I am, having to call up Pearl's devoted grandparents to tell them their girl grandbird is a boy grandbird. This did not go over well at first. My dad just kept asking for proof. My mom didn't say anything (trust me, this is highly unusual). She actually told my dad he should hang up because she couldn't speak. I began to worry they wouldn't love Pearl anymore. Then I began to worry they wouldn't love me anymore.

When I talked to Dad the next day, he pointed out that the issue he was having the most trouble wrapping his head around was how easily we had all assumed certain behaviors were specifically female in nature. The NCS people told me that in the parrot world, the male birds are the most talkative and flirtatious. Female birds tend to be much more demure. So all the traits we thought were most charmingly "feminine" turned out to be textbook male bird behaviors. This also explained why, in 12 years' time, Pearl has never once laid any "blanks" (unfertilized eggs).

Oddly, fortuitously, Pearl's name was not chosen by virtue of him being a her but due to chick coloration—both girl and boy birds of Pearl's particular coloration are all grey until the first molt, which also explains why the bird department manager initially thought he was a she. Perhaps even more oddly, however, the coloration Pearl was originally named for is apparently not the one he actually has. I now know that the pearl coloration is much more striated with closely interconnected spots of grey and white (or yellow, or both) all over the bird. According to the experts at the NCS, Pearl is a "male whiteface split to pied cockatiel." I had to write that down and store it in a file so I could remember it later.

The true miracle, of course, is that I remembered where I stored that file when it came time to write this story.

It has been more than a year now since we discovered our little feathery she is a he. I am happy to report I love him just as much—maybe even more—because love sometimes hands us challenging lessons and I have learned a lot from this experience. Pearl of course has learned nothing....which is just as it should be. My new friends at the NCS continue to remind me Pearl is not gender-sensitive even if we are. When that doesn't work, they offer me gender-appropriate name ideas to take my mind off things ("Earl", "Paul," and "Pearl Jam" are the most recently rejected submissions).

The NCS folks also continue to helpfully funnel more "proof" my way whenever I veer off again into doubt. To date, I have amassed quite a robust photo collection of other male whiteface split to pied cockatiels.

For the record, they all look exactly like Pearl.

On the Subject of Avian Selection

I often use Pearl as "Exhibit A" in my talks on healthy body image, self-esteem, and mentoring.

Because of this (and also because, like any proud parrot mommy, I see no reason to stop telling people—whether they seem interested or not—how wonderful my parrot is), sometimes I am asked how I decided to select a cockatiel for a pet rather than some other bird breed.

Consummate people-pleaser that I am, I always wish I could give these folks an impressive and well thought out scientific answer. "Well, when I was researching the flocking behavior and genetic longevity traits of *Nymphicus hollandicus* versus *Melopsittacus undulates*, I discovered..." Nope. Starting around age eight, I just kept selecting parakeets for pets. At some point, I decided to select a cockatiel for a pet instead. It was no more or less scientific than the process by which a Southern Starbucks aficionado decides it is only fair to check out this odd Dunkin' Donuts coffee obsession East Coasters have. The worst that can happen is you now have another reason to feel superior to those who drink Dunkin' Donuts coffee.

I actually like Dunkin' Donuts coffee better than Starbucks, but only because they pour the cream in for me—and they give me more cream than I would give myself. If I poured the equivalent amount of cream the Dunkin' Donuts counter boy gives me into a cup of good old-fashioned Starbucks coffee and did a side-by-side taste test, there is approximately zero percent chance I would be able to tell the two apart. And I would probably like them both very much.

This is relevant because most and perhaps all of my decisions are made with this exact same level of painstaking research and deliberation. I decided to quit my post-college job at the oil company because a voice in my head (literally) told me to quit my job and move to India. I did. It was a wonderful experience. When I was 29, my grandfather unexpectedly gave me a check for $10,000. I spent an energizing five minutes deliberating with myself before deciding to use all of that money to record an album of my original songs. It was this decision that, in a weird and wonderfully circuitous way, led me to the work I do today as a speaker, writer, nonprofit director, and mentor.

On that subject, I actually started my career as a public speaker by turning down requests to share my personal recovery story. Back then, not many people were talking about eating disorder recovery, so once other people knew I had recovered, they wanted to know how I did it. Unfortunately for them, at that time in my life I couldn't think of any career other than "exotic dancer" (never an option) that held the potential to make me feel so publicly vulnerable and exposed. Finally one particular organization attempted to lure the reluctant exhibitionist in me to the podium with a large check called an "honorarium." I decided I felt suitably honored and the rest is history.

So my point here is that I don't make decisions in a "decision-making" kind of way. I feel something move inside me, a little voice dares me, I think "how hard/bad could it be?," or something similar occurs, and then I just do it. This works for me.

However, if somebody absolutely insisted I outline for them the exact best process by which they should choose a pet parrot (as opposed to how I choose a pet parrot), I would probably tell them to first consider carefully how much time they have to spend with a pet parrot, how willing they are to train a parrot, and how excited they are about becoming their parrot's primary companion. If the answers to any of those questions are "not too excited," I would strongly advise against bringing a new pet parrot home to stay.

It is also worth mentioning here that finances can become an issue, and not an insignificant one. Parrots (like people) need lots of stuff—cages, birdseed, treats, toys, vet checkups—and these costs can quickly add up. Plus, parrots enjoy chewing...a lot. Anything that is chewable and within beak reach will likely get chewed—and the bigger the beak, the larger the chunk it can take out of the mini-blinds, woodwork, artwork, and other prized items of interior décor.

Travel can also become problematic, primarily because pet parrots (regardless of size) do not easily tolerate being left behind. As such, they are quite capable of holding grudges—for weeks, months, or forever—towards owners who "abandon" them for vacations, work trips, or any reason at all. To further complicate matters, as they reach sexual maturity, parrots are more apt to bond closely with only one person per household. In so doing, they often become jealous of other pets, mates, kids, roommates, and guests, prompting some potentially tough decisions about the household pecking order.

Last but not least, parrots typically operate on one volume—LOUD. Sometimes they will vary this with "extra LOUD" and "unbearably LOUD"—at which point housemates, neighbors, and total strangers may begin to lodge their own totally understandable complaints.

Having said all this, and for what it is worth, I will concede that I could and should have taken all of these factors into consideration when selecting a particular breed of pet parrot. I could and should have, but I didn't.

I selected a cockatiel in the same way I make all my decisions—because it just "felt right."

For Bird Lovers Only

If I'd had a tree house when I was little (which of course I didn't—I was way too clumsy to manage to hoist myself up an actual tree) I imagine this is the sign I would have hung on the door:

"For Bird Lovers Only! All Others—KEEP OUT."

Now that I'm older, I might reconsider and let other animal lovers and their non-bird, non-human companions join us.

Yet the fact remains that keeping a companion bird is not for everyone. Unlike cats and dogs, birds have not been domesticated through the centuries to readily cohabitate with humans. As a result, even many initially enthusiastic and well-intentioned bird owners have little real idea of their new pet bird's needs or capabilities.

As a lifelong bird owner myself, I often find myself explaining to the bird-curious (or bird-ignorant, as the case may be) that under the right set of circumstances, there is quite simply nothing more wonderful than cohabitating with a tame pet bird.

Imagine if you will the most creative, energetic, and affectionate kitten or puppy you've ever encountered. Then add wings. This is what you are likely to experience once you decide to open your home and heart to a companion bird that has been raised and reared to become a pet.

A Note about Wild Exotics

If, however, you elect to bring home a bird that has not been born and bred for life in captivity, you can expect your new winged housemate to be every bit as aggressive and resentful as you would be if someone suddenly plucked you from your lifelong native natural habitat and shoved you into a small lockable steel structure with a food cup, a few wooden sticks, and a tiny door.

As anyone who has watched the Nature Channel or the movie *Rio* knows, the exotic bird smuggling trade is alive and well today. Every year thousands of wild exotic birds are captured in the most inhumane manner possible and then sold to uneducated bird shoppers as "pets." These birds will remain wild—virtually untamable—until the day they die or somehow manage to escape or both (very few transplanted exotic birds who escape captivity are able to survive for long in their new, non-native wild environment).

Furthermore, attempting to tame a wild bird by force is not ever a positive experience for either bird or human. It is one I urge you to avoid at all costs. But since you currently have in your hands a book called *Love & Feathers*, I can (and will) happily assume your future plans include only the best for yourself and any avian you may choose to share your home and heart with.

Introducing the "Cockatiel"

Here, you will be reading about a particular breed of exotic (breeder-raised) pet bird, the "cockatiel."

The cockatiel is known to be a particularly friendly and lovable type of small parrot. Like parakeets, cockatiels make especially wonderful pets for those new to keeping parrots. They are easy to train, usually get along well with other pets and people, are bright and enthusiastic, and generally want to be wherever you are doing whatever you are doing.

A Note about Ownership

I feel compelled to pause here and just mention that I personally dislike the word "ownership." I have never felt like a "bird owner." I own furniture, dishware, small appliances—I do not own other beings, human or non-human. But given that one of us cleans the bird cage, provides all of the food and water, and schedules and pays for the vet visits, while the other one of us shrieks, preens, molts, poops, flings birdseed, and attempts to kill the vet with surprising regularity, "owner" or at least "responsible party" is a fairly accurate description of certain facets of my role in the relationship. However, I prefer the term "parront," as do many other parrots' human companions, so I will be using that term for the remainder of this book.

Meet Pearl

The majority of *Love & Feathers* will focus on a single representative of the cockatiel species. His name is Pearl. Pearl, like all birds both domestic and wild, is not a mammal. Rather, he belongs to a class reserved just for birds called "Aves." According to the official Wikipedia definition, Aves are "warm-blooded, feathered, winged, bipedal, vertebrate, egg-laying tetrapods." To simplify things, when people ask I usually just say he is a "bird."

Within class Aves, cockatiels and their older, larger, louder cousins, the cockatoos, are also grouped into a smaller and more exclusive sub-family called the Cacatuidae. Even though I am a spelling bee champ, I have no idea how to pronounce this. When I looked up the answer it quickly became clear nobody else does either (this made me feel better even though it didn't resolve my question.)

Within the Cacatuidae family, cockatiels then get their own sub-family (Nimphicinae), genus (*Nymphicus*) and species (*hollandicus*).

Other important facts about Pearl (aka a bird, aka a cockatiel, class Aves, family Cacatuidae, sub-family Nymphicinae, genus *Nymphicus*, species *hollandicus*):

Gender: Male.
Age: Timeless. I hope. (Typical lifespan is 20 years but the oldest known cockatiel was 36!)
Length: 10 inches (head to tail, not including crest).
Width: 2.5 inches (across wing blades).
Wingspan: Getting Aves to open wings, hold still, and get measured should be an Olympic sport. Which means we may never know.
Weight: 75 grams.
Color: Grey and white.
Favorite color: After grey and white? Green.
Favorite specific shade of green: Houseplant green.

<u>Favorite food</u>: Waffles.

<u>Other favorite foods</u>: Anything else my mom cooks or that other people are eating and not sharing.

<u>Favorite shreddables</u>: Library books and expensive store-bought books (not necessarily in that order). Magazines—and not the ads. Aves prefers the meaty editorials I am looking forward to reading. Wicker—and anything else not designed to come into regular contact with small, sharp beaks.

<u>Favorite activities</u>: Shredding (see above). Admiring himself in reflective surfaces. Showers. "Typing" on my laptop. Shrieking. Flinging seed. Neck scratches. Pooping on the carpet. "Singing" along to my soothing meditation music (at which point it is neither soothing nor meditative and not really worth the $25 I paid for the CD...)

<u>Daily schedule</u>: Rise—whenever I get up. If I get up too early (unlikely but it has been known to happen) Aves will hiss and try to bite when the cage cover is removed. All morning activities then revolve around Aves until cage changing, feeding, a shower (if desired), and location of a preferred perch is accomplished. Aves, exhausted by all the attention, then naps. For hours. Upon waking, spa services (neck massage, feather scratching) are usually required. Attendant must be prompt to avoid shrieking. Attendant must not leave Aves' line-of-sight view at any time—and definitely not the premises—while Aves is awake...or not awake. Bedtime is whenever Aves gets more tired than an extended nap can deal with (usually around sundown, or 8pm in summer).

<u>Vocabulary</u>: Shrieking. What sometimes sounds vaguely like "pretty birdie." And, of course, the special chirps that Grandma (aka my mom, aka the Small Tree, aka the Small Chef) has taught him.

<u>Favorite perches</u>: Window ledges. Shower door. Blue bathroom bucket. Near anything reflective. Any location within shredding distance of any item that is off-limits, important, or irreplaceable. Right on top of waffles, pizza, or other delicacies someone else is (was) intending to consume. The Small Tree. The Tall Tree (aka my dad, who at 6'3" is the official "approved height" cockatiels prefer).

Birdthropomorphism

Nearly every bird book I have ever read begins with some kind of cautionary disclaimer related to a long, intimidating word the author absolutely insists s/he did not do or even think about doing. This word is "anthropomorphism."

Anthropomorphism refers to assigning human qualities or characteristics to non-human things. These non-human things can include animals, plants, cars, deities (such as God, for instance), governments, weather—even furniture is not off-limits. While anthropomorphism is a potential issue in any book including humans and non-humans (so basically all books), scientist types get particularly concerned about its presence within a text meant to instruct other scientists.

So I want to make it clear right up front—just in case you are still clinging to any lingering doubts—that this is not a scientific text. This is also not a book in which you will read any research results or breaking news about birds. Rather, you will be reading about a relationship between one parront (me) and one parrot (Pearl). In relationships of course, each participant contributes what they know, which in our case is pretty much limited to what we have observed to date about ourselves and each other.

Although I suppose the observation part could be considered research, depending on whom you ask and how persnickety they are prepared to be. In scientific circles, observational research is usually called "qualitative research." Qualitative research is the kind of research where you pick something and sit and watch it. Or follow it around and attempt to ask it lots of questions. Then you start to learn things. You can pick just one thing to study, too.

In light of this new information, it appears I will be doing quite a lot of qualitative research here.

In the course of my exacting qualitative research in the pages to follow, I will contribute the lingo and understanding of a "human" and Pearl will contribute the lingo and understanding of a "bird." Since I have been elected as the official typist, I will be using all of the "human" lingo and understanding I know to tell our story on behalf of both of us. This will no doubt result in anthropomorphism. So be it. If Pearl was able to type and had been elected the official typist, AND there was a word for what occurs when birds assign bird qualities to human beings, I am sure I would be birdthropomorphized throughout.

Just for the record, so long as it comes with a shiny medal that says "honorary bird," I am totally okay with this. We birdthropomorphized folks really like shiny things.

Love–Trust–Surrender–Sufficiency–Peace–Potential

Every morning I wake up and there they are again—my six words.

This, of course, is because they are hanging on my wall. I went to Target and found this oh-so-cute art deco bird picture hanger that uses paper clips instead of a frame. I didn't need another picture hanger but it had birds on it so I bought it anyway. I took it home and hung it on the wall and those six empty paper clips just stared at me for a while.

Then one day I realized it was the perfect place to display my six words—the words I had chosen for the year to represent what I was striving towards in my life. (For the record, Pearl would have preferred those six words to read: "millet–waffles–neck feather scratches–mirrors–shredding–more waffles, toasted." But since I am the one with the job and the wallet I got to choose the words.)

Somewhere around the time I was printing out those six words and slipping each one into its little silver paper clip, I was also beginning to work on this book. Although at the time I didn't really think of it like a book—more like a collection of (really great) Pearl stories, or maybe an extra-long parrot-centric blog post. I thought to myself, "No matter what happens with these stories, I will always have them even when Pearl is no longer with me." I read them to my parents when we went to Cape Cod. We laughed together. They corrected my grammar. It was all great fun.

Then the collection of stories started to grow. In reviewing 12 wonderful years to date, I found myself surprised and delighted by how many adventures my parrot and I have already enjoyed together. Then I thought, "Man, it is totally awesome to hang out with a parrot all day. Other people will want to know about this." Then it occurred to me that maybe other people (like other parronts) already do know about it. Then I thought, "Maybe those other parronts would enjoy reading cute parrot stories, instead of always having to settle for reading stories about cute canines or felines or equines or other pets that don't have feathers."

Then I read in a magazine that, according to the Bureau of Labor Statistics, pet parents on average spend more money annually on their animal companions than they spend on retirement savings or wine. This last part I found challenging to believe, until I calculated in my head that one bottle of the finest wine I can afford to drink costs about nine bucks, and one "well-bird" vet check-up costs about ninety bucks. Ergo—there must be lots of people in this world like me who drink cheap wine so they can afford to pay for expensive "well-bird" vet check-ups...and to read (reasonably priced) books about cute parrots.

This was the pivotal moment in which my extended anthem on "Pearl the Prettiest Cutest Smartest Sweetest Parrot in the Whole World" became "Love & Feathers: the book." So here it is—an official book. A book I hope you will want to read. A book you may already be reading...

(Before I lose track of my original point completely) I also just want to say that at some point while writing *Love & Feathers* I realized my six words are just as applicable to navigating the peaks and pitfalls of parronthood as they are to navigating every other unpredictable aspect of daily life. In fact, each and every day Pearl and I share multiple experiences of love, trust, surrender, sufficiency, peace, and infinite potential. Our stories here are divided into these six categories, not so much because each story fits into only one category, but because adding more categories gave me more of two things I love: symmetry and the chance to remember and write down even more great stories about my (very) cute parrot.

So...a longer parrot-centric book and a more organized one as well. And—most importantly—a book both Pearl and I hope you will thoroughly enjoy!

A Word about Book Structure

One particularly wonderful thing about parronthood is that "aha" moment when you realize you are as much follower as leader, student as teacher.

Each day I spend with Pearl is a day I learn something new and necessary that deepens our bond. Often I say to myself, "Shannon, don't ever forget this (experience we shared, lesson Pearl taught me, et al)." But memory being what it is these days, I often find that the best way to proceed is to summarize in my journal or on our blog just the essence of whatever it is I want to remember.

So that is how I have structured the chapters in this book as well. The long-form story comes first, followed by a shorter section called "Lessons with Wings." This section is my way of summarizing–preserving–celebrating whatever little gem of beauty, wisdom, and light I have received through experiencing that particular adventure with Pearl. You may have a totally different experience than mine when you read the stories, of course—which is equally fun and wonderful!

Speaking of which, when I was younger I used to feel so jealous of people with dogs, because they seemed to have this great community of folks where they could all get together with their pets and share their love of furred beings great and small. But today, we feather-lovers have that chance too—through books, social media, clubs and associations, websites, and (best of all) swapping lots of photos and stories about our cute parrots.

All that to say, I love love love hearing from other parronts—so if you want to share your experiences of a story in the chapters that follow, or send Pearl and me pictures of you and your cute parrots, or share stories about you and your cute parrots (or cute pets of any species), you can email us anytime at:

shannon@loveandfeathers.com

<u>Part Two</u>

A Love Story in Six (Symmetrical) Parts

Love

I knew it was love the first day I set eyes on a certain tiny round clump of grey feathers thoroughly matted down with dribs and drabs of baby bird formula…and he promptly clawed his way up my arm, onto my shoulder and under my hair, where he clung to individual strands for balance as he cuddled close to my neck—for nearly an hour.

I knew again it was love the first time my seven-week-old bird somehow kept his eyes open long enough to wait for me to get home from work, crawled out of his cage into the palm of my hand, tucked his head behind his wing and instantly fell asleep.

I knew yet again it was love the first time I walked into the bathroom late at night only to discover my three-year-old parrot had had his first night fright, spraying the bathroom with enough birdie blood to make even the most strong-stomached human (and I am not a strong-stomached human) faint—and I didn't. Instead, I rushed him to the vet and even helped to hold him still while Dr. Fix patched him up.

I know it is love each and every time I close the door behind me and hear Pearl shrieking for me to COME BACK RIGHT AWAY—all the way down the street.

I know it is love when I walk back in the door and an impatient grey and white feathery someone lifts his wings and puffs up his chest and bobs his head and starts to simultaneously scream and race back and forth across the cage bars to remind me that the melting ice cream, poaching eggs and souring wine can wait...

Birdie welcome-home kisses come first. And love. Always love.

Must Love Birds

When my family and I were vacationing on Cape Cod this past fall, the weather was so beautiful that Mom and I went out walking nearly every day.

One afternoon we were attempting to take J.P. Morgan, my folks' couch-loving standard dachshund, for his afternoon drag when we met a neighbor who was also out walking her pets. She had with her two dogs and one....cat. The woman was rather advanced in years but her trio was young and spry. The cat in particular, leash-less next to the two hapless constrained canines, was practicing an escalating series of evasive maneuvers in between the legs of its housemates. In appearance, it was lithe and lean with keen green eyes and reddish-brown fur interspersed with white stripes.

Initially the woman stopped to talk with us about the weather, but the conversation quickly turned to pets. When we praised the youth and sleek attractiveness of hers, she lamented, "Yes, but unfortunately my cat is a turning into a serial killer. Yesterday he caught and nearly killed a gopher and brought it into the house. It got free. I tried to catch it, but it ran up my pajama leg and then out onto my head. As I was sprinting outside to shake it off, my cat brought in a second near-dead gopher and released it in the house."

Charming.

Yet cats continue to outrank birds on the "most popular pet list" year after year. Perhaps this is because, as one is cunning predator and the other delicious and unsuspecting prey, cats keep offing their competition. As a parront, I have been the unwilling recipient of all too many of what I call the "I had a bird once..." stories. These are the stories that start out well enough, where the happy interspecies

27

family is peacefully cohabitating together, at least until one of its furrier members falls prey to instinct or an empty cat food dish. Next thing you know, the family member with the feathers is MIA and a full scale FBI investigation has been launched, leading to the discovery of telltale incriminating clues like flight feathers near the litter box. Case closed.

This issue is not particularly relevant to Pearl and myself since "felines" routinely makes our annual list of top-ten-perils-to-avoid. Where it becomes a bit more challenging is in the world of online dating, when a potential match neglects to mention a critical lifestyle preference—for instance, owning a cat.

Don't get me wrong. As of the moment I'm penning this chapter, I have not yet met a "potential match" (this is what most online dating sites call their victims) for coffee or otherwise where the sole clear disqualifying factor has been the presence of a household feline. The one who used methamphetamines was an easy no in my book, as was the one who confessed on our first (and only) date to a raging case of obsessive-compulsive disorder, after which he proceeded to scientifically measure and then cross-check the portions of wine he poured for each of us. Similarly, the one who arrived an hour late and then spent the rest of our date explaining in great detail why any woman should be grateful to wait for him and the one who scratched his balls for a solid hour while consuming multiple martinis were both out.

As of this moment, actually, online dating itself has been out for quite some years now, and has already been pre-added to future years' top-ten-perils-to-avoid list. This preventative safety measure was instituted after my (hopefully very) last online dating date, when my date shared over twin steaming pots of custom-blended organic tea how much he loved his two indoor cats, and how, as he watched them eyeing the songbirds in the trees outside, he worried that by not letting them out to chase and kill the birds he was depriving them of "quality of life."

I thought briefly of depriving him of quality of life before I decided I would miss Pearl too much while in prison.

So instead, I cancelled my online dating membership and used the refund money to buy my small feathery guy a few crunchy new birdie chew toys and a delicious pack of fresh "original" flavor millet stalks.

After all, Pearl and I found each other—at a moment where the very last goal on my mind was to fall in love with a new baby parrot.

If it can happen once, it can happen again—as long as I am willing to trust in the timing of all good things....and good people who must love birds.

<u>Lessons with Wings</u>: *Love never lies. As it turns out, Pearl's presence in my life is an excellent litmus test for the people I invite into my life. Pets, like kids, are transparent—they like you, or they don't like you. If I catch myself thinking, "my bird wouldn't like such-and-so," or if Pearl hisses and pecks at a visitor instead of his more customary single-bound leap forward onto even the rankest stranger's outstretched finger, that is a sign I should pay attention to—and do.*

Soulmate, Size "Small"

When I was a girl, I dreamed of meeting my soulmate. He would be dark and handsome, not tall exactly, but at least as tall as me. He would be funny, kind, smart, affectionate, understanding, and my best friend. As of this year, I am 42 and still searching.

Sort of.

Common definition upholds the "soulmate" as a person's other half. There are a variety of theories about this. One colorful legend states that the Greek gods punished their power-hungry, four-armed, four-legged, two-faced (as in two faces on one head) human counterparts by splitting them in half. At this point, the humans' desire to rejoin with their literal other halves quite naturally superseded their desire to heft the royal trident and hurl lightning bolts. Fast forward a zillion years and things haven't changed much. Current pop psychology continually cautions lovelorn singles against thinking a soulmate union will offer much beyond non-stop and fairly painful opportunities for self-improvement.

In my own ongoing quest for the requisite self-improvement (I figure while my soulmate is still busy making himself scarce I might as well use the free time productively) I have read everything from *If the Buddha Dated* to *The Mastery of Love, He's Just Not That Into You* to *Codependent No More*. While each has added greatly to my overall intellectual knowledge of how humans date, mate, procreate, and separate, their impact on my tangible singleness to date has been negligible. Unless, of course, you factor in the inverse effect all this reading is having on my personal fervor for actually finding my soulmate.

I say this because apparently dating is hard work. First, you have to find the person. Then you have to figure out if they like you. Then—if you pause long enough in your headlong dash towards the platinum ring to complete this step—you have to figure out if you like them. Then you have to try to get your timelines in sync (frequently this step involves the much-maligned "biological clock.") Then you have to survive the wedding. The honeymoon. The in-laws. The pets. The kids. And each other.

If you are lucky (and the statistics aren't lying) your romantic bliss will carry you through the first year. The next four years will be a fairly even mixture of "what have I done?" and "who the heck did I marry?" The fifth year you will either split or start marital counseling...or both.

All of which has conspired to ensure that the more I survey my placid, uneventful, and insanely uncomplicated solo life, the more I appreciate what I have.

Plus, I can't help but notice I already share my life with a certain feathery dark (grey) and handsome, funny, kind, smart, affectionate and understanding someone...someone who also just happens to be my best friend.

Lessons with Wings: *In the Jewish tradition, one Yiddish word for soulmate means "destiny." But nowhere in anything I have read to date does it specify a soulmate has to be your same species. Pearl and I have been through so much together and yet, unlike so many other relationships in my life, we are still together, still surviving, still thriving. If that isn't a textbook happy case of reunited soulmates, I don't know what is.*

A Muse is a Muse No Matter How Small

I love it when new people first walk into my home. This is not because it is so neat and tidy (although often it is, which is mainly because I find cleaning easier than writing) or because it is so spacious and well laid-out (which it clearly isn't). Nope. It is because of the birds.

Recently my neighbor came into my casa for the first time to share some news. In her words, "Wow! You have a lot of birds!"

Yes I do. Like variations on a particularly excellent theme, I have bird key racks, bird picture frames, bird pillows, bird stuffed animals, bird-on-a-wire wall decals (amazing what you can find on Amazon), bird photographs, bird paintings, and of course bird. As in the real live feathery kind.

This is what happened. Not being particularly skilled at or enthusiastic about interior design for its own sake, when I moved into my new home a couple years ago I took one look at all those blank walls and decided I needed a theme. I was familiar with muses already from my years as a musician and then my years as a writer and basically all my other years as well. In fact, I had always wanted a personal muse, but until I realized muses could be avian as well as human it didn't occur to me I already had one.

Once I brought myself up to speed the decorating just flowed. Then others (Mom) pitched in. Then word got out that if a person wanted to buy me something for a housewarming present I would probably like it much better if it had a bird on it somewhere. As a bonus, this has also kept overall home decor costs quite reasonable to date.

But the truth is, muse or no muse, gifts or no gifts, being surrounded by birds just makes me happy. It doesn't matter what kind they are either (although Pearl prefers to keep the house hawk-free, which I find perfectly understandable). And since "happy" translates to "productive" and I am my own work-from-home boss in a company of one, the happier I am the better my (self) performance reviews also tend to become.

Recently a few friends have entered my house and commented that there are "birds everywhere." To me this is simply stating the obvious, but their tone occasionally seems to imply a "less is more" approach might be better received. To their point, the other day a fellow member of the National Cockatiel Society posed this question to our Facebook group: "When do you know you've crossed the line from being a bird lover to being a bird hoarder?" I thought this was a terrific contemplation—for someone else.

As for me, as long as I have a heart that beats (and a bit of free wall space) there will always be room for one more bird.

Lessons with Wings: *There are so many things in this world that can trigger sadness, anger, or other less easy-to-feel emotions, but the presence of birds will never be one of them. Through my love for Pearl, I have learned that when I choose to surround myself with people, animals, and images that reliably evoke joy, I can also count on feeling more joy each day of my life. And I definitely want to feel more joy!*

It's a Bird! It's a Plane! It's a Bird!

Recently I went on vacation to the East Coast. I was very excited about this for a number of reasons, including the plentiful supply of award-winning beaches, the legions of tiny cute sea hermit crabs who live in their waters, and the chance to sneak away from my nonprofit, speaking, and writing duties for a while.

But mostly I was excited because I was finally going to get the chance to plow through my stack of unread bird books. Some people like to spend their vacations climbing mountains or taking salsa lessons on the beach. I like to spend mine immersed in all things "bird."

Bird Sense: What It's Like to Be a Bird by Tim Birkhead was at the very top of my to-read stack. This is because I have been waiting to find out the answer to this question since I turned seven.

Before I started reading *Bird Sense*, I was convinced I would discover within its pages the long-buried origins of my own inner bird. Unfortunately, I discovered nothing of the sort. Rather, reading completed, birds now seem even less like birds and more like superheroes (aka as unlike me as possible).

An example—birds have a "magnetic sense." Using their magnetic sense, birds can figure out how to get from point A to point Z when they've never been to Z before. Then from Z they can find their way back to A again without making a single wrong turn. Ever.

I can't even get from point A to point B without a GPS system and a detailed map. And that is just for the places I've already been to before.

Birds can also see in ultraviolet light. So all those scientists who theorized about the biological function of fancy feathers on dude birds apparently neglected to check out the visual appeal of ladybirds when viewed through a set of UV-enhanced eyes. Bird eyes also have extra individual super powers. Basically, one eye sees up close and the other sees far away (which eye does which gets set up while the bird is still in-egg). Once set, both eyes see with 20/20 vision—whether they are in motion or at rest—for the balance of the bird's lifespan.

In contrast, I have prescription glasses to help correct my oh-so-not 20/20 vision. Yet even with their help I still squint at the picture on my "big screen" television (which is located approximately six feet away from my comfortable stationary couch).

Birds also possess a sense of hearing, taste, touch, emotion, and probably lots more superpowers we don't even know about yet. But perhaps the most amazing superpower birds have is the ability, as Birkhead says, to make us "fall in love with birds."

That they certainly do.

<u>Lessons with Wings</u>: *I have become increasingly conscious over the years of just how easy it is to assume non-human beings are less intelligent, accomplished, or aware than human beings. I have also realized how much I miss out on in my relationship with Pearl when I make this assumption. In bringing Pearl into my life, I possess the undeniable advantage. While I try hard to meet him halfway, the burden still falls to Pearl to follow my schedule, learn my language, and interpret my instructions. I can only imagine how challenged I would feel if our situation were to one day be reversed, and I suddenly found myself up in the trees with a set of wings, a beak, claws, one close-seeing and one far-seeing eye. I only hope that on a daily basis I show Pearl as much patience and encouragement as he would need to extend to me if he was the human and I was the bird.*

Power Pooping

In general, I have found people have lots of questions about parrots.

Parents want to know how much care they will require (and whether their seven-year-old can handle it). Neighbors want to know when the shrieking will stop. Landlords are quite naturally concerned about the preservation of crown molding, mini-blinds, and overall household aesthetics.

But when you wade through all the questions and all the curiosity, what it all inevitably boils down to is poop.

Specifically, how much do parrots poop? How often? Do they poop on people? Deliberately? Can they control their bowels? (This last from a former landlord, a man who used to live with a cockatiel and was clearly suffering from poop-related post-traumatic stress disorder.) The answers are "a lot," "often," "hard to say (but I suspect yes)," "see previous question," and "it depends."

Of course, the bigger the parrot, the bigger the poop. But here size can work to a parront's advantage, because a bigger bird is also a smarter bird, and smarter parrots (like smarter people) don't tend to prefer walking over, sitting in, sleeping near, or otherwise routinely encountering the product of their own hind ends. Specifically, I have heard stories of African grey parrots, a species perched at the very pinnacle of the parrot intelligence spectrum, telling their parronts they need to poop, pooping only at certain times of day, or relocating to the same single sequestered location each day to poop.

As a parront, I think this is nothing short of brilliant. As a parront to a cockatiel, this also means I suffer from a perpetual case of poop envy. My bird, being both smaller and less discriminating than those finicky African greys, takes a somewhat different approach. If he has to go, he has to go. Whatever is underneath him at the time—my hand, my laptop keyboard, the carpet, a houseguest…is fair game.

Then there is the whole issue of poop analysis. Avian veterinarians can get quite intense on the topic of what proper parrot poop should look like. Unfairly culled from a limited pool of perfect poopers who consume a carefully controlled parrot diet, these "sample droppings" bear approximately zero resemblance to what the typical parront observes exiting the typical parrot on a daily basis.

So parronts are then faced with one of two choices. Option A: rent the empty office space next door to the vet so as to expedite daily poop examination, or Option B: assume parrot poop (like people poop) can vary tremendously from parrot to parrot, poop to poop, and day to day.

For instance, Pearl is what is known as a "power pooper" (a technical term invented by his mommy). Through the wisdom of his DNA, which strives to keep him as light as possible for flight, he has no built-in "holding tank" in his physical makeup.

So basically, he poops fast and frequently. When I pick him up, he poops. When I put him down, he poops. If anything startles, excites, or frightens him, he poops. He poops before eating, during, and after. He poops at takeoff and landing. He can poop in his sleep. His poop is the reason I have tissues and paper towels stashed between the couch cushions, beside the desk, and in all the cabinets.

Although, frankly, I rarely remember to use them until it is, um, too late. As one book states, "Everybody poops." Some poop more often than others, and some poop more publicly than others, but in the end, it's just poop.

And my parrot is worth it.

<u>Lessons with Wings</u>: *When I brought home my first parrot at age eight, I was already unconcerned about poop. Three decades later, nothing has changed. Through my relationship with various companion parrots and most recently with Pearl, I have learned love*

doesn't see poop. Love sees love. When I look at Pearl, I don't see a pooping parrot. I see my companion, my friend, my heart.

I Love You, I Love You, I Love You

Cohabitating with a parrot is like having a self-esteem therapist come and live in your house with you.

For starters, there is the behavioral modeling. By this I mean, who can (or wants to) argue with someone who thinks they are that wonderful, pretty, and smart?

And then of course there is the praise.

I love you. What a BEAUTY you are! Mommy loves her angel bird— love love love! What a SWEETheart my baby is! So smart AND so pretty—Mommy is so lucky! Who is Mommy's beautiful birdie? Such a pretty PRETTY BIRDIE! Where's my favorite—where is Mommy's FAAAvorite? Awww...there he is...Mommy's absolute favorite! Mwah! Mwah! Mwah! (Insert multiple belly kisses here).

See what I mean?

Here I have noticed that while at first the human psyche is crystal clear about who is doing the praising and who is being praised, after a while that line can start to blur. A lot. This is significant because the typical parrot response to praise tends to be enthusiastic repeat requests for more praise. Ergo, one round of endearments can rapidly multiply into 10 or 100 rounds before you know it (who ever said repeating daily affirmations couldn't be fun and easy?).

Research too supports this theory. Social scientists tell us we tend to become like the five people we spend the most time with. As any parront knows, a parrot is just a smaller person with wings and feathers instead of hands and hair. So if the person we spend the most time with can't get enough of his or her own company—and ours—well, even the most robustly pessimistic self-regard may in time cave in the face of such unrelentingly positive peer pressure.

Finally, it is not without significance that the oh-so-obviously praiseworthy parrot in question too has flaws. Let's take Pearl for instance. We can start with the pooping—constantly—in the most inconvenient places and on the hardest-to-clean things I own. And then there is the shrieking...always the shrieking. As well, a self-confident parrot can with little (or no) provocation morph into a biting parrot, in service to re-establishing household "dominance" over that insignificant being with the much bigger brain and the bank account who does all the scrubbing, feeding, washing, and (of course) praising.

Yet somehow, despite all the pooping and shrieking and pecking and the rest, the praise continues. This just goes to prove that both praiseworthiness in general and the individual being praised in particular has little to do with what we do and everything to do with who we are. When I praise my parrot, I also praise my own love for him. I praise my wisdom in selecting a parrot to be my close companion. I also praise my selection of this particular parrot who has taught me so much and trusts me with his life. And I praise this tiny miraculous feathery being who unashamedly loves himself just as much as I love him.

And who wants me to unashamedly love myself just as much as he loves me.

<u>Lessons with Wings</u>: *I have long believed that crowds—a phenomenon often dismissed as stupid—can also be quite smart. In fact, the whole premise of the nonprofit eating disorders mentoring organization I founded several years ago, MentorCONNECT, is based on the hypothesis that putting together a group of folks who each individually wants to recover will have the happy side-effect of bolstering the whole group's recovery progress as well. To date, I am happy to report our growing community has consistently proved*

me right. In a related experiment closer to home, I have also discovered that whether the crowd is made up of two or 200, one individual's high self-esteem can be positively "catching" for the rest. For example, every day I spend with Pearl I feel even better about him...and me...and us.

Alex and Irene

"Alex and Irene"—it sounds like a love story, doesn't it? And it is a love story of sorts.

Alex represents, to date, the world's greatest known avian intellect. Irene, aka Dr. Irene Pepperberg, is the woman who trained him and fought for recognition of not just his specific abilities, but for the implied abilities of parrots as an entire species.

Alex—short for "Avian Learning EXperiment"—is the African grey parrot the world at large fell in love with in varying stages throughout his life. For some, the sparks flew right away during the tumultuous early years of his training. For others, the love story began as results from the preliminary *Alex Studies* proceeded to overturn decades' worth of prior scientific theory about avian intelligence.

For still others, their tender feelings for the smart grey and white bird were kindled only after his untimely death from a heart arrhythmia at age 31, as wave after wave of worldwide publicity eulogized his achievements. Alex's final words, spoken to Irene on the night before his death, were, "You be good. See you tomorrow. I love you."

If my bird could speak in human language, I would imagine these are the exact same words he has been saying to me every night for the past 12 years.

Far in advance of any expressed interest from the mainstream general or scientific communities, Dr. Pepperberg first captured the hearts of parronts everywhere when her research into the cognitive abilities of her crew of African greys validated our own less scientific yet still viable impressions of our companion birds' abilities. Irene's work with Alex & Company proved parrots have the emotional intelligence of a two-year-old human child. Intellectually, parrots can compete head-to-head with a child around the age of five. The *Alex Studies* proved again and again that yes, parrots can think. Yes, they can speak—in both words and other vocalizations. But most importantly, they can comprehend that of which they speak.

What this means for parrots today is that they are at last being recognized for the intelligent, creative, empathetic social beings they already are and always have been.

Not surprisingly, Dr. Pepperberg is one of my personal mentors and heroes, as she is for so many parronts. Not unlike myself as I struggled to overcome an eating disorder and ultimately succeeded in doing so against what felt like overwhelming odds, Dr. Pepperberg had to lose nearly everything before the value and impact of her work with Alex was finally embraced by the scientific community and beyond. Her marriage, her home, her funding*, her peace of mind, and her heart (never more so than on the morning Alex was discovered dead on the floor of his cage)—all were up for grabs in what seemed like the great impossible race to test, validate, and publish before it all crumbled down around her.

Yet somehow, she kept going. Somehow, her vision for the possibilities of interspecies connection, communication, and learning sustained her in times when certainly nothing else was presenting itself as sustenance. Somehow, in the mysterious way of great beings with ground-breaking missions to accomplish, her epic battle on behalf of avian intelligence and quality of life was fought and won with little more than a small office, a handful of volunteer graduate students, a computer, certainly a radical new testing protocol, a hefty dose of vision, one trained research professor, and a feisty grey and white parrot.

Alex and Irene, on behalf of parronts and parrots everywhere, Pearl and I simply want to say "thank you...for everything."

*During the course of her work with Alex, Dr. Pepperberg established The Alex Foundation. The Foundation's mission statement is "to improve the lives of parrots worldwide." To learn more and contribute to Dr. Pepperberg's ongoing work, visit: **www.alexfoundation.org**

<u>Lessons with Wings</u>: *People are smart. Some people are smarter than others, and some of us are smarter in different ways than others of us. In the same way, parrots are smart. Some parrots—and some parrot species—are smarter than others, and different parrots are smart in different ways. Even though cockatiels are not the "talkers" in the parrot species, and certainly are not considered to perch at the highest end of the parrot intelligence spectrum, I can (and often do) draw so many parallels between my parrot's behavior and the behavior of my young niece and nephews—not to mention my own behavior at times—that I have never once doubted Pearl's intellect. Perhaps this is also why, to me, Dr. Pepperberg's work with Alex is fundamentally a work of respect. I share my home and my life with another being who, in his own way, is every bit as emotional and intelligent and responsive and consciously alive as I am. I count myself supremely fortunate I am aware enough to notice, appreciate, and honor this fact!*

In Search of a Ladybird

There is no delicate way to say this. Spring is the season for lovers.

As well, it would seem that the "spring effect" exempts no one—whether they happen to have fins, fur, flippers, a shell, bare skin, or feathers. When spring arrives, the sentient mind naturally turns to thoughts of love.

And to making an egg, if you happen to be an avian.

The first hundred (thousand) or so times I witnessed my feathery sidekick attempting to make an egg on his own I wasn't sure what I was observing. Or maybe I just told myself I wasn't sure. The appreciative chirps, the repetitive body motions, the "wind down"—it all looked a bit too much like the "birds and bees" lecture we got in seventh grade biology—except that particular chapter never mentioned witnessing the phenomenon in one's 12-year-old pet parrot.

I didn't have definitive proof until last Easter when, while browsing up and down Target's "Easter specials" aisles, I spied a cute pink felt Easter basket with an even cuter felt applique of a yellow chick on it. I filled the basket full of soft plastic "straw," packed in some goodies and headed over to my folks' house for our traditional Easter morning brunch. My mom took one look at the basket and said, "You must take that home with you for Pearl—he will love it!" I was quite sure he wouldn't love it.

Yet again, I was wrong. The basket was barely emptied of chocolates, jellybeans, et al, before it was occupied once again. This time, the contents included 75 grams of grey and white feathers emitting distinctly territorial body language. I took the Easter basket home with us and hung it on the side of the chair where Pearl's cage sits during the day.

After which Pearl commenced to "nesting." Each day he would clamber up and over his cage and down the other side, sling his body through the back bars of the chair and ricochet down into the soft straw. Then he would start chirping—not the usual raucous shrieks I get, but soft, sweet, actual melodious chirps that sounded...well... romantic.

And the search for a ladybird was on again.

To date the success rate has been low. Perhaps it is because parrots are not the most patient of creatures, and maybe five minutes of alluring chirping is not enough time for a single ladybird to make up her mind. More than likely, however, it is simply because we do not have any ladybirds here at Casa Feathers n Beak. The nest is soft and cozy and in a great, safe, family-friendly location. The occupant is resourceful, self-confident, attractive, and healthy.

But there are no ladybirds within a several mile radius.

A definite plan glitch if I've ever heard of one.

Lessons with Wings: *Sometimes I worry that by not bringing a second cockatiel—a female this time—into our home, I am depriving Pearl of the chance to mate and have a family of his own. Yet as a parront I also realize I am not well equipped to take on the challenge of caring for an entire family of cockatiels. Instead, I strive to be present for Pearl each day and to be as active and interactive a companion as any pet parrot could want. We both do the best we can to make the situation work. This is all any parront—or any parrot— can do.*

If You Love Something Make Sure It Doesn't Get Away

Parrots don't give their love in half measures. Where this trait often becomes especially evident is when there is a desirable item up for grabs.

Even after its former owner has made it perfectly clear the desired item now absolutely, totally, 100 percent belongs to the parrot, the parrot in question will often still take additional measures to certify ownership. Take Pearl, for instance. Let's say I am about to enjoy a delicious grilled cheese sandwich. I have already planned to reserve a portion just for Pearl. In fact, I have already done so. I have even moved his portion to the corner of the plate nearest to Pearl so he can clearly see it is his.

But if, during the course of our meal, my breath or hand or arm hairs or immortal soul happens to venture into range of "his" portion (or my portion for that matter) I will find myself on the receiving end of an open beak and a warning hiss.

This is because there is no such thing as simply "staking your claim" when you are a parrot. You first stake your claim. Then you stand on top of it. Then you attempt to ingest as much of it as possible as quickly as possible. Sometimes—if an item is especially desirable—you also poop on it just to make sure even those who still wanted it badly no longer do. Not surprisingly, this technique is fairly foolproof.

One odd area where Pearl in particular shows a surprising degree of non-attachment is when it comes to his own feathers. As long as the feathers remain on the bird, any attempt to groom, pluck, clip, or otherwise alter said feathers will be swiftly and decisively repelled.

However, once a feather has molted off my parrot's body, it then becomes both gone and as quickly forgotten. Sometimes I pick up an especially lovely freshly molted feather to admire—and then I show it to Pearl. He hisses at it—but not in a "come closer that's mine!" kind of way—more like a "go away and take that scary grey alien with you!" kind of way. Clearly, once a feather has made its decision to secede from the union, the split is both unforgivable and irrevocable.

Luckily, this is not the case when it comes to parrots and parronts. Parrots who are bonded with their parronts are also unwaveringly loyal. Here is proof. Pearl loves my parents. He loves them so much he often pretends I'm not there when he is with them. But if I walk out of the room—well, all I can say here is I hope at least my folks' parrot-related hearing loss is even in both ears. Pearl will start shrieking loudly and continue until I return to the room. The moment he sees me, he will go right back to pretending I don't exist.

He is even like this at home when he and I are the only two beings in the house. He will pretend I'm not even there—like he is thoroughly enamored of the view from his window ledge or the shiny guitar toy with the bells his Grandma gave him. This can go on all day as long as I am sitting quietly on the couch or at my desk chair—well within line-of-sight. But the moment I head for the kitchen or the laundry room or outside to get the mail—well, at this point any neighbor who has ever wondered "is there an actual live bird in there?" will get real-time audio confirmation.

The instant I reappear, however, the shrieking stops. Pavlov would be proud. But not as proud as I am of my sweet, loving, loyal, shrieking parrot.

<u>Lessons with Wings</u>: *In a culture that appears to thrive on daily doses of contrived competition with the continual threat of rejection and abandonment as a motivation to strive for success, unwavering lifetime loyalty is not to be taken for granted. There is a reason I can't imagine life without a parrot companion. Even if I have had the*

suckiest day imaginable—even if everybody else hates me—even if Pearl should also hate me because I just took him to the vet again— in my parrot's eyes I am wonderful. I am that singular someone he loves so much he will go to any lengths to make sure I don't ever, ever, EVER get away.

I See You

If you are an introvert like me, a parrot is a great pet choice.

Simultaneously independent and needy, commitment-phobic and clingy, a parrot's idea of a perfect day is to do whatever they feel like doing—totally unencumbered and of course undisciplined—without ever once having to endure any actual solitude.

Like humans who visit "dude ranches" so they can pretend to be cowboys, parrots seem to take singular pleasure in playing at self-sufficiency—at least until they get hungry, thirsty, sleepy, or their neck feathers start to itch. Then, of course, it is always the right time to return to the "ranch house" for some five-star victuals served up in air-conditioned comfort...followed by a neck massage to work out the aches and pains from all that wrastling or wrestling or whatever pretend cowboys do all day on pretend ranches.

The truth is, even the most domesticated of parrot-parront pairings (here I am thinking of Pearl and myself of course) functions best when neither party pretends there is any bona fide autonomy going on. This way, no one gets bent out of shape when one partner breaks line-of-sight and the other partner shrieks loudly in protest. No one expects to actually have a whole (or even part of a) waffle all to themselves. No one feels the need to ask for awkward repetitive permission before pooping in public yet again. Nor does one totally independent party ever think to complain about the ongoing not-optional chore of scrubbing the other totally independent party's poop out of the carpet yet again.

Speaking of being independent-yet-connected (well sort of), not long ago I watched the movie *Avatar* for the fourth or fortieth time. In the film the humans greet each other by making up tasteless jokes about disabled Marines being "meals on wheels." In contrast, the Na'vi native people greet each other with the respectful "I see you."

While I did struggle a bit to comprehend why producer James Cameron didn't include more parrots in what is clearly supposed to be an otherworldly version of paradise, I didn't have any trouble understanding why the humans wanted to take over the planet—or why the Na'vi didn't want to give it to them.

I also didn't have any trouble understanding what "I see you" meant, although some other people apparently did. The moment the film was released, scholars and bloggers began to hypothesize in long form about the meaning of "I see you." Some folks have said it means until you are seen by someone else, you technically don't exist (yikes). Others have claimed it means the god within one person is greeting the god within the other person (which of course makes me wonder what the two actual people are saying to each other while their two gods are chatting it up). Still others have proposed that it is more like a confirmation—when one person says "I see you" and the other person responds in kind, both people can then know they are both there...which I suppose can be helpful in certain situations.

All that to say, it is obvious to me none of these budding philosophizers is also a parront.

If they were, they would also already know that "I see you" is simply a condensed way to say, "I love you—you're so pretty—you're the one—you are the sweetest bird in the whole world—what a love—Mommy loves her birdie—this one is my favorite—how did Mommy get so lucky—you are my angel—what a good bird you are—what a pretty, pretty bird...."

<u>Lessons with Wings</u>: *Thanks to Pearl, I will never go a single day without hearing the words, "I love you." I will also never go a single day without saying the words, "I love you." This is because every day I spend with Pearl is another great day to say (and hear) those precious three words: "I love you."*

One Trick Parrot

Some parrots can recite famous verses and sing whole songs on command. Others can ride skateboards, dance, create art, solve math problems.

Pearl does none of these things.

He is neither graceful nor rhythmic. His short-term memory skills rival mine (this is not a compliment). His grasp of mathematics begins and ends with the concept of "subtraction," which occurs whenever I attempt to remove the waffle from his plate before he is finished consuming it.

In all fairness, Pearl's Mommy can't do any tricks either (unless you count touching my toes, which my 6'3" father reliably marvels at each time I achieve it). But then again, unlike Pearl, I am rarely asked what tricks I know, nor do I seem expected to supplement my scanty existing repertoire just to entertain others. If someone is really bored and wants a quick laugh, they can just present me with a recipe and join me in the kitchen.

There is one thing Pearl is very good at, however. Prettiness. Whether it is admiring prettiness (any even mildly reflective surface will do), enhancing prettiness (molting, preening, showering), sharing prettiness (few beings enjoy being center stage like my feathery angel), or simply living by example, Pearl eats, breathes, and sleeps prettiness. He sees prettiness whether he is looking especially pretty or not (molting does no parrot any favors).

For Pearl, prettiness is a state of mind and a way of life. Those who look at a small grey and white parrot and do not perceive prettiness are in need of education, not condemnation. Pearl is always happy to help with this.

I feel prettier too—just by being around him. Factoring in the daily substantial hours we spend together, I wasn't at all surprised recently when my folks told me they both agree I am looking prettier than ever.

For the record, it didn't require much of a search to locate my personal shrieking fountain of youth.

<u>Lessons with Wings</u>: *It is a rare being who—just by showing up— can make others feel prettier, happier, more at home in their own skin. We can change our body, our job, our partner, even our whole life, and yet still feel sad or empty on the inside. In fact, I tried all of this to no avail before I met Pearl. Now, my heart leaps each time I enter Pearl's presence, both at the sheer exuberance of his love-filled greeting to me and mine back to him. To love and be loved— that is the question....and the answer to all questions.*

Trust

Trust is….

When you have to get your claws trimmed, your beak smoothed and your wings clipped—and you eventually actually agree to hold still and allow the vet do all three totally unacceptable procedures, but only after Mommy has given you many reassurances and multiple kisses on top of your soft feathery head.

Trust is…

When there's been another hawk sighting (and you know this for a fact because you are the one who saw it) and you first take time to shriek a warning to your "flock" (aka Mom) and only then take shelter (under Mom's hair of course—this is always the safest place).

Trust is…

When you "step up," even when you want to do anything but (i.e., the grout was very tasty or the mirror was very shiny) just because Mom asked you to…and Mom always knows what is best for you.

Trust is…

When you are quiet and well behaved so long as Mom maintains direct line-of-sight, but turn into a shrieking feather fest the moment she disappears. Then, when she returns, you instantly become quiet and well behaved once again.

This is trust in a parrot's world. And in a parront's world as well.

Bring Your Bird to Work Day

"Is this an office or a zoo?"

My co-worker, Jeff, can be heard muttering ominously out loud to himself in the next room.

Once again, it is bring your bird to work day, and except for periodic mad solo dashes to the little girl's room, Pearl and I are joined at the beak as I bottle-feed him from my desk until he can be weaned.

I think any person who can behold the sight of my bird's tiny grey feathery body perched in my palm, small soft oversized pink baby beak wide open to receive dribs and drabs of formula, without their heart melting is a cretin. Jeff thinks any employee who brings their pet to work is a former employee.

Luckily, Jeff is not my boss. Equally fortunate is that our mutual boss, Lynn, is understanding of my predicament. While a baby bird is not quite apples to apples when compared with a baby human, Lynn is at the moment a single mother juggling a high powered career, three dependent youngsters, a collection of demanding higher-ups and of course the hostile being in the office one over from mine. All of which has conspired to ensure "yes" was the easiest answer to, "Can I bring Pearl to work instead of having to run home all day long to feed him baby bird formula for the next two weeks?"

Really, with all the trouble going on in the world today, why the heck not.

But even Lynn is starting to get restless. Far from the unobtrusive featherweight innocent I described (I may have even promised "you'll never even know he is here") Pearl, newly removed from his even more hostile flock mates, simply cannot abide being left alone. Ever. Short of moving my desk into the restroom, wearing diapers, or installing a catheter (believe it or not, by this point I've actually considered all three) the entire office is being forced to endure punctually timed shrieking sessions when Mommy's bladder overflows yet again.

And forget browsing the office café for lunch—for me "bring it from home or starve" is my governing motto these days. Not to mention that there is some unsubtle jealousy percolating as other employees imagine how nice it would be to have Coco or Fluffy licking their toes under the desk as they pore over boring spreadsheets or take calls from grumpy soon-to-be-former customers.

It is clear I am receiving special treatment from our rising star of a new boss and everyone else is eager to take me down a peg or two. But Pearl doesn't care—and frankly, neither do I. Every time I look into those wide round soft black eyes and see that tiny beak open up for more formula, I just melt. Jeff can be as venomous as he likes.

I have the antidote and a newfound mission in life—to make sure this precious and defenseless creature lives to see tomorrow morning.

<u>Lessons with Wings</u>: *Now that I work from home I can look back at those office days and realize just how inhospitable many of today's workplaces are for the human beings who have to work in them. I spent years sitting under the glare of neon overhead lights, coping with unattractive and noisy surroundings, dealing with disgruntled coworkers and inadequate break times, all the while doing my level best to hide the fact that I also had a life that didn't involve my job description. Never again. I know now that what I need to be both happy and productive is flexibility and integration (together with a healthy side helping of feathers). In other words, only when my personal life and work life are permitted to meet and mingle can I maximize my chances of success with both.*

The Dreaded V-E-T

It is that time again.

All I have to do to know for sure is to offer my fluffy sidekick a finger perch. I wait. He climbs up and clamps on for the ride with all five claws and I am not even wasting time imagining what it would feel like if he possessed all eight. Five is plenty bad enough. But the pain I feel right now is nothing compared with what is about to happen next.

Dr. Skip Fix has been Pearl's vet since he was a downy bottle-fed chick. It is Dr. Fix I call at midnight when Pearl has had a night fright—again—and the bathroom looks like Freddy Krueger just paid us a visit. It is Dr. Fix who meets me on a Sunday morning at seven a.m. sharp when Pearl's wing has kicked out yet another impacted blood feather. Dr. Fix is also the one who pulls out his Rolodex for a specialist referral when need be.

Most recently, Dr. Fix's Rolodex led us to Dr. Fronefeld, the avian surgeon who was called in to consult about ongoing issues with Pearl's left wing. Damaged from birth, likely from bullying by his older and stronger nest mates, Pearl has never been able to grow out his left wing's long primary flight feathers—feathers that are critical in allowing him to maintain altitude for flying. Consequently, he "flies like a rock" as my dad often jokes. He also has a lot of trouble folding that wing back, and sometimes spends ten minutes or more trying again and again to refold it into a comfortable position after a "flight."

While the injuries Pearl sustained as a chick has gifted him with an unusually sweet and loving disposition, they also represent an ever-present and lifelong danger to his health. Following his periodic molts throughout each year, several irregularly formed pinfeathers sometimes attempt to simultaneously crowd through his left wing's single half-functional primary flight feather follicle. If left untreated, night frights, bleeding out, and even death are potential outcomes. While this "perfect storm" situation doesn't occur every year, it has been getting worse as the years go by, and the feather follicle is at this point red and severely inflamed.

Dr. Fronefeld impressed me right from the start when he somehow managed to restrain my angel inside of a birdie-sized x-ray machine.

Miraculously, he not only got Pearl's tiny wriggling feathery body and both wings inserted into the device, but he also made Pearl hold still long enough to capture on camera evidence of a) exactly how best to treat his once-again swollen and bleeding left wing tip, and b) clear visual proof I am living with a real live modern-day dinosaur ("Pterodactyl" would be my guess). During the x-ray process Pearl screeched loud enough for drive-by passersby to hear, but Dr. Fronefeld remained unmoved.

I am thinking the good doctor must be deaf.

When we left the vet clinic, Pearl was sporting a bright green wing bandage and accompanied by an expensive vial of pain medication that smelled like old dirty gym socks (although clearly it tasted better than it smelled because Pearl guzzled it down the way I guzzled down one or several vodka tonics later that evening). I, on the other hand, was sporting a deep and primal maternal guilt complex that appeared to range all the way back to the Age of the Cave Mama, even though I was not yet in the picture when Pearl's siblings inflicted their early nest violence and thus could not have defended him back then.

While routine vet visits are not usually as traumatic for either parrot or parront as trips to the avian surgeon, each visit does have its predictable challenges. The first challenge is the car ride to get there. Pearl has never been a particularly peaceful passenger, which I can certainly appreciate when I view the trip from his perspective. In my role as "driver," I have a comfy cushioned seat with built-in shock absorption, a seatbelt that fits me properly, and I get to drive, adjust the temperature, and pick the music, which means I am in control.

Pearl, on the other hand, has to cope with a cage that rattles loudly enough to drown out the various shakes and sighs of my eight year-old Toyota, and his "seatbelt" is a modified bungee cord I bought for $0.95 at the local hardware store. But Pearl makes sure the ride is as miserable for me as it is for him by employing his signature series of escalating pathetic peeps and panicked shrieks. These are accompanied by restless wall-to-wall pacing across the floor of his cage and useless climbing up one side of the cage, across the top, and down the other side again. Some days there is so much noise and activity in the front passenger seat of my car that the hectic highway route we have to take to get to the vet's office appears almost pastoral by comparison.

When we finally pull up in front of the clinic I experience a momentary reprieve. This is because Dr. Fix is also a parront—to a yellow and white cockatiel named Goofy. Goofy has one working leg. Pearl has one working wing. They are kindred spirits separated at birth and they know it. Their bond is instantly rekindled the moment I bang open Dr. Fix's front door and Pearl hears the shrill call of a willing avian co-conspirator with whom he can strategize. Even the free-range cats that roam the office grounds offer no cause for concern once Pearl and Goofy recommence to plotting their escape.

Their hopeful attitude quickly fades, however, when Karen the vet tech appears.

Now we enter the phase of the visit I call "catch the cockatiel." Bad wing notwithstanding, Pearl has a number of ingenious maneuvers he uses to attempt to evade not one, not two, but three individuals who are intent on restraining him, two of whom are highly trained for just such an exercise. On the books is a physical exam with vitals check, claw clipping, wing feather trim and beak smoothing. Pearl loathes all four procedures and is absolutely determined to prevent any of them from taking place. In the same way a human being who couldn't bench press his way out of a paper bag somehow manages to muster superhuman strength to lift a whole car up and away from a child trapped beneath it, Pearl reliably "finds his wings" in the exact moment his cage bottom first encounters the hard metallic surface of the exam room table. I have seen him actually launch himself out of Karen's hands and make a break for it—impossibly attaining both altitude and velocity in the process.

The only part of the visit Pearl doesn't mind overly much is the weigh-in. He has a choice—stand directly on a shiny platform (under which sits a small scale) or climb inside the lidded weighing globe balanced on top of the scale—this piece looks not unlike the vessel E.T. traveled in to get to Earth back in the 1980s. Since the shine factor is high for either option, the weighing—which nearly always returns a reliable verdict of "75 grams"—goes relatively smoothly.

The rest of it....well, let's just say eventually Dr. Fix and Karen win rounds three, four, five, and six of "catch the cockatiel," the targeted extremities get examined, trimmed, clipped, groomed, and smoothed, and a very subdued Pearl is once more deposited into his cage, where even the sight and sound of a still-energized Goofy fails to rouse him as we exit the building.

He will stay like this for several hours, rubbing it in that Mommy is a bird murderer and he has clearly escaped by the skin of his beak yet again. No amount of millet, crunchy toast, fresh-made waffles, or even the juicy forbidden leaves of a bright green houseplant will rouse him until he deems his sulking has adequately made its point.

<u>Lessons with Wings</u>: *True love includes tough love sometimes. It is very difficult for me to put Pearl through his checkups, but if I say those three little words ("I love you") I'd better be prepared to back them up with actions to show I mean what I say!*

Traveling Girl

Birdseed? Check. Millet? Check. Waffles? Check. Sunflower seeds? Check, check.

I am standing beside Pearl's open cage, bird in hand. Belly kisses? At least 100. I'd better give him a few more just to be safe.

We are on our way to Ray's, where Pearl will be staying at my breeder friend's posh birdie hotel once again while I embark upon my fall travels. I fly first to Oklahoma and then to Illinois to speak at two different girls' conferences, and then on to Cape Cod where I will join my folks for what (I hope) will be a restful, relatively internet- and phone-free vacation getaway. I told my dad last week I feel like the Energizer Bunny at that critical moment when the little wind-up thing on his back finally begins to run out of steam. I just hope I get to the vacation part of my trip before it winds down completely and stops.

This vacation has been a long time coming. But there is just one hitch. I can't take Pearl. I have often wished for a pet that travels well, but Pearl isn't it. In fact, if he couldn't stay with Ray, who, with his zillions of professional singing canaries, mustache parakeet, and assorted avian others, is singularly well equipped to take in yet another diminutive Type-AAA avian as a lodger, I probably wouldn't ever go anywhere.

It doesn't help that Pearl is the kind of bird who doesn't enjoy being left. Luckily for him, I am the kind of parront who, despite my innate Sagittarian love for exploring, doesn't like leaving him. To this end, whenever we are necessarily apart, I cope with the separation by making sure the rest of my life oh-so-casually broadcasts BIRD! From the tree o' birds appliqued to the back of my

MacBook (so I won't mix up my laptop with somebody else's at the airport, of course) to the screensaver of a proud (and very pretty) grey and white cockatiel on my phone, it is clear to even the most casual of observers that there is just one special parrot in this traveler's life.

But none of this helps ease my mind on the night before I drop Pearl off at Ray's. I suppose this is also where it becomes unnecessary to mention I have never reproduced. At age 42, my eggs are old and tired, so these days I happily channel whatever is left of my maternal instincts in the direction of a certain very receptive avian. When I have any extra instincts left over, I change the water in my fishes' bowls and water the plants (which probably explains the rather erratic success rate I tend to have with each).

During the short drive to Ray's, Pearl clings to the side of his cage, pressing his feathery body so close to the cage bars I suspect he is trying to sneak through one feather at a time. At traffic lights, he poses like a cover model when I train my iPhone camera on him, using every ounce of his considerable storehouse of cuteness to convince Mommy to LET HIM OUT PLEASE. Unaccustomed to being caged, he is understandably irked when I fail to respond to his increasingly unsubtle hints. He alternately sticks beak, then feet, then tail through the cage bars, making it obvious the current situation is utterly untenable by avian standards.

Finally, we arrive. I unhook Pearl's "seatbelt" from either side of his cage and lift the whole contraption out of the car. He screeches. While I wait for Ray to answer the door, Pearl paces, running from one end of his biggest perch to the other. Once inside, however, the chirps emanating from cage upon cage of twittering birds captivate him, and when I finally do open his cage door to let him out, he immediately clambers up my arm, onto my shoulder, and under my hair, finding a secure vantage point from which to survey the lay of this new bird-rich land. Sarah, Ray's gorgeous diva of a mustache parakeet, screams out a few choice words of self-praise by way of welcome, "Sarah is a pretty bird! Step up! Good girl! Sarah is a good girl!"

Pearl sees Ray and clings even more tightly to the skin of my shoulder. As well as being the birdie hotel owner-manager, Ray is also the official beautician for both residents and guests, in which capacity he handles any necessary manicures (wing trims) and pedicures (claw clippings) that may be needed. Unlike image-conscious humans, however, image-conscious avians are not typically quite so fond of their stylists. No matter how many years Ray of Ray's Birdie Hotel has been taking care of these oh-so-routine, safety-oriented grooming tasks as needed, Pearl still reacts to the occasion by assuming everyone in the room, Mom included, has suddenly decided to kill him. While I am typically quickly forgiven, Ray has not been so lucky. Pearl deigns to sit on his finger, but refuses to let Ray scratch his neck feathers or pet him.

I attempt to distract Ray from Pearl's appalling lack of manners by pointing out the vast array of bird treats I have brought with me. I explain I have mixed up Pearl's preferred special custom blend of birdseed, millet, whole grain cereal, and extra sunflower seeds in one bag, and I have also brought an extra full bag of plain millet stalks for him just in case. But Ray has moved on to other matters, and is now worrying out loud to me about the thick file folder of instructions my mom recently delivered to him regarding proper care of my dad's Father's Day present, Boyd.

Boyd is a crown tail betta fish. In place of the usual long, arcing tale that most male bettas have, Boyd has what looks like a fantail of tiny waving anemone tentacles. He is a beautiful sight, gracefully weaving and winding through the water of his small tank as he navigates between the fronds of a blue and green plastic "plant." Ray opens the binder to show me where Mom has highlighted, bolded, and even triple underlined certain key passages.

Boyd is named for Boyd Crowder, a character on the television show *Justified*. My parents love *Justified*, and they love Boyd. I tell Ray he is lucky they are only leaving their fish and not their dachshund, J.P. Morgan, in his care. Morgan would have arrived with an entire file cabinet's worth of instructions, as well as a cyanide tablet for Ray should Morgan happen to expire while under his care.

With that, it is time to go. Ray is en-route to a bird show, where he will serve as the celebrity guest judge for yet another high stakes statewide canary contest.

And if I don't go now, I will unload every bit of my luggage and eschew two lucrative speaking gigs and a well-deserved five-week vacation to stay at home with my favorite bird.

<u>Lessons with Wings</u>: *It is always difficult for me to entrust Pearl to someone else's care—even someone so capable, qualified, and bird loving as Ray. Yet self-care (like working to earn rent money and taking vacations to rest) is a priority I must not neglect if I want to be fully present and available to care for Pearl, too.*

A Very Good Bird

Lately I have gotten in the habit of asking Pearl, "Are you being a very good bird?"

Like "fuhgeddaboudit" for mobsters and "whatev" for teens, I have found this open-ended (and highly rhetorical) question is effective when applied in a variety of scenarios.

For instance, let's say my tiny hookbill is doing something extra cute. Here, a sugary sweet singsong rendition of "Are you being a very goooood biiiiiird?" clearly conveys both full parrontal approval and license to continue.

But then let's say a certain feathery someone decides to pursue known off-limits activities. Here, a sternly issued, "Are you being a GOOD BIRD?!?!" accompanied by swift avian relocation measures can quickly and firmly reestablish the household pecking order.

Or so I'd like to think.

I feel it is important to point out here that on no occasions when I ask Pearl this question is he actually being a good bird. This is because a) none of his favorite activities ever makes the good bird list, and b) very good birds (like very good people) tend to bore the socks off us both. For both of these reasons I expect neither of us to be very good very often—if ever.

As it turns out, this might actually be a good thing. One of my favorite books is *The Four Agreements* by Don Miguel Ruiz. While I don't always understand everything Ruiz teaches, one concept I have no trouble grasping is a process he calls "domestication." In Ruiz's Toltec tradition, domestication is what happens when human beings teach other human beings how to talk, act, and fit in (in short, to "be good"). Ruiz calls these lessons, which start the day we are born, "agreements." When the lessons first begin we learn to agree with our teachers about which behaviors are acceptable and which behaviors are unacceptable. As the instruction continues, we also work out agreements with those around us about who we are, who we are not, and who we can never be. Once we learn each lesson well, we become fully domesticated and can then turn around and teach others what we've learned.

As you can probably already imagine, the domestication process often hurts. A lot.

Another favorite writer, Brene Brown, PhD, has done a great deal to bring to light the culture of toxic shame that pervades our lives today. She writes about how shame is a favorite tool to socialize us to accept cultural norms. So is blame. So is punishment (physical, emotional, relational, financial, and so forth). So are many other painful things.

On this same topic, Ruiz talks a lot about how much of the pain of domestication comes when we decide others' unloving perceptions of us, and our own of ourselves, hold water. In other words, after repeated exposure to the same messages again and again, we can (and often do) actually begin to believe we are socially awkward, inept, fat, ugly, stupid, unwanted, a failure, any and/or all of these things.

In my own life, attempts to domesticate me led to a 15-year battle with an eating disorder, followed by another 10 years of crippling depression and anxiety. In order to recover I had to question and revise so many concepts I had picked up about myself. Even today I sometimes still have to work hard to fight off lingering impressions of where I "fit" in the overall social scene, what I can and cannot ask for from others, what I do and don't deserve, and so much more.

Happily, my avian suffers from none of these ailments. For his 12 years to date, Pearl has stubbornly resisted all efforts towards domestication. Pearl is who Pearl is. Pearl wants what Pearl wants. Some people who meet Pearl love birds. Others don't like birds and still others are afraid of birds. Pearl doesn't take any of it personally. Pearl looks at the whole world like a giant fun parrot play station and every being he meets as a potential new friend. He is not domesticated and he most definitely is not "good," or at least not in the way the domestication-minded amongst us might define goodness.

For this, I am truly thankful.

<u>Lessons with Wings</u>: *Watching Pearl fling himself towards daily life with total disregard for social niceties gives me a whole new perspective on where "goodness" fits into the big picture of being alive. There are so many definitions of the word "good"—everything from "moral" (blah) to "well-behaved" (yawn). My favorite definitions are "honorable," "genuine," and "real." Pearl is all of these things. With his help, I am continually striving towards the same.*

The Art of the Parrot-Proof Home

Ha. As if.

I say this for a number of reasons, but mostly because parrots find everything interesting...and I do mean everything.

If you have it, they want it. If you have it and don't want them to have it, they want it even more. If it is so dangerous or toxic that you must not ever allow them to have it, you might as well sprinkle sunflower seeds (or millet or waffles) all over it. I know this is true because every parront I've ever met has a horror story of rounding the corner just in time to discover their avian beak-deep in that-thing-they-must-never-have, which (of course) is located smack dab in the center of the so-called parrot-proof portion of the home.

This is probably also the right moment to mention that the whole concept of parrot-proofing anything is a figment of humans' overactive imaginations. Parronts dream of it, strive for it, live for it. Parrots casually cast it aside the way teenagers discard Santa Claus and the Tooth Fairy (although even the hardened mature amongst us never quite seems to give up on Cupid, which is a topic for a different book). The point is, in the wild a parrot's naturally curious, inventive, intelligent mind is a great asset. In captivity, it usually just gets them in trouble.

Speaking of captivity, recently a captive cockatoo named Figaro (a cockatoo is basically a larger, louder version of Pearl) stunned Austrian researchers by making a tool to nab tasty cashews deliberately placed just outside his enclosure. The researchers went, er, nuts, putting the so-called breakthrough video out on BBC Nature and issuing erudite statements like, "It's almost as if he [Figaro] discovered a solution and then managed to apply it." Duh. They could have just come to my house and filmed Pearl trying to evade my attempts to evade his attempts to dismantle my laptop keyboard yet again. My tiny hookbill may lack the same level of manual dexterity for actual tool making that his bigger feathery cousins have, but the building blocks are clearly all there.

So with actual parrot-proofing out of the question, I have had to pull a Figaro to keep one of us out of trouble and the other one from having to double her anti-anxiety meds. For example, I have found that choosing a small casa really helps. Not only does this keep rents manageably low, but it is hard for Pearl to get into too much trouble when the only way to break line-of-sight is if one of us closes our eyes. Also, as a general rule of thumb, when I am not home Pearl stays in his cage, and when I am home, Pearl is wherever I am (luckily, he also prefers this, so he helpfully alerts me if I happen to forget). Finally, wherever an off-limits item exists (and there is no option for removal or camouflage) I just make sure there is an even more desirable approved item nearby for him to enjoy. It works every time.

Or nearly every time.

<u>Lessons with Wings</u>: *Kids will be kids, and parrots will be parrots. In other words, as long as dangers lurk in the world, inquiring human and avian minds will encounter them (and occasionally even seek them out). No matter how excellent my parronting skills may become, I can't prevent every bad or dangerous thing from crossing Pearl's path. But I absolutely can do my best to always be there in case he needs my help to emerge from the encounter safe and sound.*

Pet-Owner Lookalikes

I love pet-owner lookalikes.

Not only do I truly enjoy giggling at the sight of people who look just like their pet pit bulls or Chihuahuas, but I wouldn't be the honest person I am if I didn't admit I can relate. Slight and skinny in my upper body, long-necked, pear-shaped, and perennially surprised, with streaks of alternating color and round wide black eyes (okay, dark brown in my case)...clearly, I chose the right pet for me.

As well, I have discovered time and again that our lookalike resemblance continues far beneath the skin. For instance, over the years it has become clear that my official parront's job description absolutely includes daily mandatory reassurances such as "don't worry" and "pretty! oh very pretty!"—words of wisdom every human and non-human being can benefit from. So our conversations, while rarely deep in the way that human-to-human chats can be, are reliably beneficial and very enjoyable for both Pearl and me.

In fact, I am often unclear about just who needs whom more. On the one hand, as the official parront, I am the registered supplier of birdseed, treats, vitamin supplements (not my most popular offering), spring water, toys, neck scratches, grooming, vet visits (definitely not my most popular offering), as well as being the entertainment and overall wellness committee chair. On the other hand, Pearl, as the official parrot, is in charge of shrieking, pooping, molting, flinging his food (and mine), shredding, preening, napping, and providing continuous companionship.

I think we both got a pretty good deal.

One thing that always surprises me is how few of my friends seem to be able to relate to the love between a human and a bird.

Some of my friends are actively afraid of birds—so much so that one gal I know refuses to enter my house at all if Pearl is there (obviously she doesn't come over very often). Others simply congregate off to one side as far away from the bird cage as they can get. Given the square footage of each of my homes to date, usually this means they have to stand on the porch. One of my guy friends— a dog fanatic who has installed tiny figurines of a dog he does not own all over his sprawling and expensive home—actually grimaced one day as he watched me kissing my feathery guy. "EWW," he groused. "I can't believe you are kissing a BIRD."

Yet record numbers of these very same people exhibit the exact same behaviors with their own (and others') beloved and much-spoiled non-avian pets. Depending upon which "official" sources you consult, the most popular pets for North Americans to date include fish, cats, and dogs—not necessarily in that order—with birds holding their own in a consistent third or fourth place from list to list. Here it is probably worth mentioning that I also cohabitate with fish (freshwater) and a variety of unidentified houseplants. Houseplants didn't make any of the "popular pet" lists I consulted, which I find odd since the mortality rates I have observed to date clearly suggest they require customized, diligent, expert care.

Pearl and I also possess a quite similar disposition. Nervous, high strung, with a palpable dislike for early hours, loud noises, spicy foods, and crowds, I keep waiting for a famous movie producer to call and suggest we co-star in one of those movies where two beings crash into each other and each wakes up as the other. I'd like to try life with wings. I think I might even be good at it. And Pearl could get a much better grip on my (his) grilled cheese sandwich if he had fingers instead of feathers.

But in lieu of this option we still have no trouble thinking up activities to enjoy together. In fact, Pearl and I have a surprising number of mutual favorites. Waffles, books (for reading and chewing, respectively), television programs or CDs that include bird calls or flute noises, anything shiny, Asian takeout featuring rice or noodles, riding around on people's shoulders (although I will admit I am a bit big for this activity now), showering, napping in the sun...there are people couples who aren't this compatible.

Not to mention we each display a noticeable preference for the other's company. In fact, it is an unwritten rule in our household that one of us (me) must always maintain line-of-sight contact with the other one (Pearl). Should one of us (me) forget this rule, even if it is just to go wash the birdie towels in the machine downstairs, the other one of us (Pearl) shrieks loudly to COME BACK RIGHT NOW! After a separation, his greetings are so reliably exuberant that even if I wake up grumpy or come home in a bad mood, I find it awfully hard to stay irked at the sight of a small (and surprisingly strong) clump of grey feathers trying desperately to squeeze himself through the cage bars to get to me faster.

We also divide up household tasks remarkably well. For instance, during the day most days, my job is to run my nonprofit, MentorCONNECT, and to write. Pearl's job is to sit on my knee/shoulder/ladder/window ledge and nap. He reminds me to take breaks by pooping on the rug. (It is brown and a rental, like the house. The landlord prefers for it to remain poop-free—hard to understand but what can you do.) When I get up to clean off the poop, I often also notice I am hungry or thirsty. Then I have to find a snack—preferably something humans and avians can enjoy together. And then before I (we) eat I can stretch out my hands and arms so I don't get hand pain from typing all day.

It is a clear win-win.

Over the years I have come to truly believe there is a "best pet" for everyone. I also deeply believe we each have an obligation to tune in and consider which animal companion is the best fit for us before making such an important choice. If you don't know which animal is best for you, sometimes it can be good to spend time with friends' pets to see what resonates. In my specific case, I have always somehow just known that "bird" is the right choice for me. I have worked hard over the years to develop a better understanding of overall animal behavior, which has included overcoming a longstanding fear of dogs (mostly by sitting on the couch petting my parents' people-worshipping, nap-happy dachshund, J.P. Morgan) and I have even uncovered a grudging appreciation for cats...or at least the ones that don't like to hunt birds. So maybe I'm still working on that one.

But put a bird in front of me and something deep and instinctual within me switches on. It is like there are little invisible "inner wings" that begin to flap in my heart. There exists a kinship I can't explain that I have never felt with any other species (even my own in most cases) and it is a bond I didn't pursue or work for. It just is.

I don't know if everyone who cohabitates with beloved pets feels this way about their animals, but I know I do, and it is the absolute best feeling ever when you find it within you.

<u>Lessons with Wings</u>: *This example clearly shows me that my instincts don't lie. I knew by age seven that I was supposed to share my life with companion birds. I never doubted this inner guidance— not once. I sometimes (often) wonder how much more of the same trustworthy inner guidance I might have access to if I spent less time doubting and arguing with myself and more time simply tuning in and trusting what arises.*

Plate Surfing

Plate surfing should be an Olympic sport. In a cockatiel's world it probably is.

In Houston where I live we have a great number of food trucks. Food trucks are like very focused restaurants on wheels. Sometimes the city plans "food truck festivals" and when these happen lots of food trucks and lots of hungry humans gather in one place and then the humans "food truck hop" from one food truck to the next, sampling the culinary treats each has to offer until they are stuffed.

Plate surfing works similarly. Only instead of food trucks, there are food plates. And instead of just hungry humans, there is also a very hungry and very curious avian. In fact, in some ways plate surfing is like a cross between a food truck festival and a baseball game. Here, it can be helpful to visualize the food plates as "bases." Each plate might have the same victuals, or there might be something different from one plate to the next, depending on what each member of the family feels like eating for that particular meal. Either way, the goal remains the same—to visit as many "bases" as possible and make sure you taste all the good stuff on each plate before the meal ends or the other diners get wise to your plan. As well, some diners are not all that keen to share their meal plate with a parrot, unbelievable though it may seem. These diners represent a special challenge to the skilled plate surfer.

This is also why plate surfing is the most fun when one or more diners are known to be pushovers. In our family, whether Pearl and I are at home alone or we are over at the Tall Tree and the Small Tree's (aka my mom and dad's) house, we are all pushovers. Regarding the matter of one very small and very cute featherweight family member, we don't have one good strong backbone among the lot of us. Mom will ask me, "Hey, do you want to come over for brunch?" I'll answer, "Sure—sounds like fun." Then Mom will say, "Well, what does Pearl want to eat?" "Waffles," I'll reply. "I have two recipes—crunchy or fluffy. Which one would Pearl like better?" is Mom's next question. "Let's try fluffy." So fluffy waffles it is. Mom will also set out some fresh-cut fruits and scramble up some eggs for good measure—just in case Pearl feels like having a bit of egg and fruit with his waffle.

See what I mean? Pushovers.

Pearl will often start out surfing choice portions of waffles, grilled cheese, scrambled eggs, pizza, pasta, or other favored items from the Tall Tree's plate. This is because, as my dad is the tallest member of the family and is thus regarded as the most favored perch, Pearl is usually already sitting on top of his shoulder when a meal begins. As well, as the family patriarch, Dad usually gets served first with the choicest portions, so all Pearl has to do is slide down Dad's shirtsleeve and walk across his hand in order to hop right onto his plate to claim the desired items. Once done at Dad's plate, Pearl will usually surf over to Mom's plate next to pick out a few more select tidbits, and then finally he will make his way towards my plate to round out the meal. By the time he reaches my plate, he is often full and simply wants to request a neck scratch or a relaxing post-meal nap on my knee.

Which of course I give him. You see? Pushovers.

Lessons with Wings: *Watching Pearl plate surf day after day, it is interesting to reflect back on the painful years I spent avoiding family meals and food in general. To have such innocent trust and enthusiasm for tasty things—to so totally dive into the gustatory experience with all senses on full alert—to even be willing to sport several days' worth of pink neck feathers (yet again) because Grandma's gourmet pizza is so completely worth it—all of this speaks to me of a pure appreciation for the gift of life that food, and good company to share it with, truly is.*

It Had to Be You

I love asking people who are in love, "so how did you meet?"

This question not only guarantees an interesting answer but pretty much exempts me from having to say anything else for the remainder of the evening. What I have learned from this is that most people seem to enjoy our conversations a lot more when they do most of the talking.

Another fascinating question I like to ask people is, "so what is the worst date you've ever been on?" I've noticed no one ever seems to have trouble answering this question. If they have been in the past or are now currently signed up for one of those online dating services, they sometimes don't even wait for me to ask the question before they start answering. What I have learned from this is that no one forgets a lousy date.

I can state from my personal history that this also applies quite well to pet encounters. For instance, I still recall myself as a tiny girl with springy black curls leaning down to pet a tiny dog with springy white curls. I also remember the tiny dog's gleaming sharp white teeth reaching out to chomp down on my tiny wrist. As with people who develop their mate, date, or pet "type" based on past bad experiences ("no women with green eyes," "no men taller than five foot nine," "no dogs with springy white curls") I decided that very day that (as far as pets go at least) the "dog" was not for me. Similarly, I remember my first encounter with a cat. It just sat there on the neighbor's lawn, looking so calm and serene, glaring at me out of evil-looking yellow almond-shaped eyes. There I remember thinking usually people at least get to know me first before deciding they hate me that much.

Interestingly, my first encounter with winged things was not avian but man-made. Specifically, I fell in love with helicopters. I used to stand in the center of our driveway, craning my neck back as far back as I could to watch them passing by. Helicopters were such curious things, impossibly propelled as they were by some odd type of circulating overhead fan. I wanted to ride in one so badly. I loved the idea of flying—of somehow being able to lift myself above the earth, to enter the realm of wind and rain and sun and clouds and sky and just float free.

Every summer Mom would take us kiddos to Massachusetts to visit her folks. Dad would join us when he could, but often it was up to Grandmom and Grandpop to entertain my brother and me so Mom could catch a break. One summer when I was eight we went on our usual summer trek, and one particular morning all five of us ended up in the central town square on Plum Island. There was a black antique wrought iron bench…picturesque red and white alternating cobblestones…and an entire flock of soft round grey pigeons. Somehow I ended up sitting in the middle of the bench with the whole group of pigeons clustered in close around me. They were at my feet, on my knees, sitting on my hands and shoulders. Then one landed on top of my head.

I was riveted. I couldn't believe these winged things—who were so free and could go anywhere they wanted to go, including places where I absolutely could not follow them—would choose to land right on me. They were so trusting. They were probably also quite hungry and I had bread, and I am sure they had lots of practice spotting a sucker when they saw one. We sat like that for quite a while, at least until they had consumed every last speck of my breakfast. When we got back to Houston in the fall I started lobbying my folks for a pet bird. Not too much more time went by before my birthday arrived and my first pet parrot, a yellow and green chatty parakeet I named Perky, joined our household.

Perky was just the first verse in what has now become a decades-long sing-a-long series (avians, like humans, love a good sing-a-long) set to the music of the hit show tune, "It Had to be You."

<u>Lessons with Wings</u>: *As I get older, I find it increasingly important to pay attention to those rare moments in life when my destiny oh-so-casually reveals its own hand. Flying. Music. Words. Birds. These have been constant themes in my life since I was small. Today, at 42, I have recorded two albums of original music; I travel frequently (usually via plane, although not yet by helicopter); I write for a living, and my home is filled with birds, including one hand-painted original portrait, which is of Pearl by his mommy, of course (see "Paint Your Pet" for more about that!).*

What Parents and Parronts Have in Common

To my mind, there is literally nothing better than hanging out with a petite feathery sidekick all day long, day after day after day.

In lieu of producing kids of my own or working with kids, serving as a parront is the next best recipe I have found for sustaining eternal youth.

In fact, when I listen to tales of new parent woes—the crying fits, the temper tantrums, the early a.m. and late p.m. wake-up calls, the mess—all I can think of is "Pearl." Often I am hard pressed not to jump in to commiserate, being all too aware of how oddly touchy new parents can sometimes be about direct infant-to-parrot comparisons.

The urge to draw parallels doesn't end when they get bigger, unfortunately. The picky eating...the repeated requests for five more minutes...the reason-free rebellions...the refusal to take part if it's not fun...the endless full volume querying and questioning centering around absolutely everything...this pretty much sums up the daily lives of every parent (and parront) I have ever met.

Yet we keep signing up for it again and again. Why? Perhaps we are suckers for punishment, or what often feels like intensely conditional love. Maybe we just like a good challenge. But mostly I remain convinced it is because of those round black (or blue, or brown, or green, or hazel) eyes staring up into ours with such trust. Our boss might think we suck. Our mate may blame us for their bad day (or bad year). Our friends perhaps persistently fail to live up to their job description.

But when the resident willful, stubborn, spoiled, and oh-so-special dependent is polled, we reliably rake in the five-star ratings again and again. What have we done to deserve this? We showed up. We combined an egg with a sperm. We pointed and instructed the underpaid sales clerk, "I want that one." We opened our wallets. We opened our homes. We opened our hearts. We opened our lives, rearranged, made room, made choices, made changes, and made it work no matter how hard (i.e., impossible) it was.

We put up with the pain, the poop, the price tag, the improperly fitting chef's hat and maid's uniform, the pecking, the puking, the preventative medicine that does everything except prevent. We made it work because it is worth it—more worth it than anything and everything else, period, the end.

Which means that in the end, what parents and parronts really have in common is, well, everything.

<u>Lessons with Wings</u>: *In reference to my parrot's behaviors, sometimes people say, "I don't know how you can stand (whatever it is)." I often don't know how either. But I do know if I focused on that one thing—whatever it may be on any given day—I wouldn't be able to stand it. So I don't focus my attention there. I focus my attention on the connection, the trust, the shared learning, the joy, the laughter, the companionship, the love. These aspects outweigh all the rest. They making parronting Pearl the best thing about my life and the pure privilege it is.*

Reflections on Prettiness

I have spent a good chunk of my life seeing myself as not-pretty...not to mention not-smart, not-successful and not-popular. Not surprisingly, what life has reflected back to me has often tended towards more of the same.

So cohabitating with a being who sees the exact opposite in his mirror each morning has been nothing short of life-changing. In a nutshell, life with Pearl couldn't get any prettier, and—at least if you ask him or his proud mommy—neither could he.

In fact, it is a rare being who escapes an encounter with Pearl without realizing what a difference healthy self-esteem can make. Secure in how he looks and who he is, Pearl simply cannot wait to share himself with others. He eagerly expresses his preferences, assumes everything is meant for two (even if it is located all the way across the room and on a total stranger's plate), calls incessantly for companionship when (rarely) left alone, and loves nothing more than to start each day by allowing Mommy to scratch his neck feathers for however blissfully long he wants them to be scratched.

In this, he offers no excuses, rationalizations, or apologies. There are no battles to conceal his genuine expressions of childlike zeal beneath a carefully maintained façade of detached grownup decorum. Accusations of arrogance or—even worse, narcissism—never come up. Perhaps because he is a parrot rather than a featherless biped, he is allowed to enjoy just as much personal prettiness as there is to enjoy, free from gossip, envy, or condemnation. When he encounters feathery peers, they enjoy prettiness together—their own and each others'. Sometimes I can almost translate the chirpy dialogue—"Oh! You're prettier! No I'm prettier! No you're prettier! We're both so very pretty!"

After which everyone concurs and gets back to scouting millet, scoping out mirror space, and grooming their neighbors' neck feathers (the better to maximize group prettiness, of course).

Parrot-to-parront conversations, too, frequently revolve around this interesting and uplifting topic. Personally, I can't remember the last time I greeted a friend by asking to borrow their compact mirror and admiring myself in it, but in a parrot's world this is considered a perfectly acceptable—and quite heartfelt—greeting. After all, the friend showed up to see you—ergo, you must be very pretty (and great company) or they would have called someone else for coffee/wine/wing-woman for their scary first date from Match.com.

The truth is, Pearl—like me—has a choice in how he views himself. But unlike me, he doesn't know it. So it just makes sense he chooses to see maximum prettiness every time. So his left wing damage means he can't do the full version of "heart shaped wings" like the other cockatiels (when the long flight feathers on each wing tip grow out and the bird lifts up both wings in unison to form a complete heart shape when viewed from behind). He is not just unconscious of this difference, but also completely uncaring. So he is considered a "petite" male cockatiel in a world of robust crests and chests. As far as Pearl is concerned, "petite" is the best size to be!

So where I have spent years dissecting my foibles and flaws, he has spent an equal number of years admiring and appreciating his strengths, attributes, and assets.

If I had a choice—which I now know I do—I know which perspective of myself I choose to adopt going forward!

<u>Lessons with Wings</u>: *The world—and its inhabitants—are chock-full of opinions. Sometimes those opinions are supportive and encouraging. But sometimes they just tear us down. It is so important to learn to tell the difference! I have found that keeping company with a (very pretty) feathery mentor can be especially helpful for correctly discerning which is which.*

Parrot Breakfast

For the first three decades I cohabitated with companion parrots, daily feedings were simple.

Every morning I would drag out the bag of birdseed, scoop a few tablespoonsful into the parrot food bowl, add a millet sprig, and then congratulate myself for being such a conscientious parrot mommy.

When I turned 41 (and Pearl turned 11), Pearl's grandma bought us a membership in the National Cockatiel Society. Since then, nothing about our daily routine has been the same. In fact, there is no daily routine. There is only the endless ongoing effort to entice my parrot to ingest sufficient quantities of nutritious, non-seed edibles.

For a time I attempted to prepare something called "parrot chop" (see "Adventures in Chop" to find out how well that went). Parrot chop is a nutrient-rich mixture of dietary essentials parronts assume parrots might seek out and enjoy in their native habitats. After months of purchasing expensive raw delicacies that neither of us enjoyed, I finally had a key aha moment.

During our mutually uncomfortable "chop era," Pearl had taken to visiting my breakfast bowl each morning—the better to avoid ever having to visit his. During these morning treks, I witnessed him willingly consuming exotic items like watermelon, papaya, Swiss chard, banana. I also observed how, when I offered him a new delicacy held between my fingers, he would often at least take a nibble—even while avoiding the very same item sitting at that very same moment in his very own breakfast bowl.

This ushered in a new morning ritual—"parrot breakfast." I work from home, so often people call me in the morning thinking I'll have time to chat before I start my workday. When I tell them, "I can't talk right now because I have to do parrot breakfast," it is not uncommon for them to just keep talking. This is because they have no idea what parrot breakfast entails. Parrot breakfast starts the moment I get up and ends at an indeterminate period of time later (basically, whenever the parrot in question either finally feels full or becomes grumpier than Mommy's patience can tolerate).

If you have ever been to Vegas and played that game where you bet on a random number on a spinning wheel, you would be a natural for parrot breakfast. The principle is similar: hold one item, then another, at beak-side level in front of your parrot's irritated face while attempting to calculate the statistical odds of consumption. If your gambling streak weighs more towards the "high risk" side, you could start with an unknown quantity—say, raw kale—that is very healthy but which your parrot in the past has avoided the way he avoids hawks and wing trims. Here, you can gamble that hunger and/or curiosity will eventually stack the deck in your favor.

Then again, if you are like me (i.e., leaning as far towards the "low risk" side of the spectrum as possible) you might prefer your first breakfast offering of the day to be a known past winner—say, a piece of hard-boiled egg. Here, the house has a clear advantage, but you may not get to bet on anything else that day since the diner's documented affinity for the proffered item makes withdrawing it ill-advised at best.

Either way, the one and only sure thing you can count on is that at some point each day your parrot will eventually consume something. And when he does, you will congratulate yourself on striking it rich....yet again.

<u>Lessons with Wings</u>: *Parrots, like people, often have strong preferences. And like people preferences, parrot preferences often develop over time and are not so easy to replace. Yet, as we have continued "parrot breakfast," Pearl has slowly begun to consume many new healthy treats. Over time, he will likely sample even more. For this big win I credit two things: my parrot's trust, and my own patience to allow him to take the transition at his own pace.*

Surrender

There is no such thing as "surrender" in a parrot's world. There is only survival...and whatever you have to do to make sure you last beyond the next encounter with the thing coming towards you that thinks you look exactly like lunch.

There is no such thing as "surrender" in a parront's world either. We might say "I surrender" but we don't really mean it. Even if we are in battle or under siege, even if someone says to us, "The only way you and your parrot will get out of this alive is to surrender" we might say the words, but we still won't be surrendered on the inside. Rather, we will be fighting every moment—strategizing, seeking a way to ensure our own survival and the survival of those whom we most love. Human beings didn't grow such big frontal lobes by wimping out at the first sign of a fight. Our survival instincts are very strong—which means we will only actually say "I surrender" when we have every intention of doing anything but.

For parrots and parronts alike, surrender only becomes a reality when it relates to what those in recovery communities like to call "living life on life's terms." For instance, perhaps my parrot might prefer an unlimited all-day toasted waffle buffet. But his veterinarian, his scale, and the entire National Cockatiel Society membership tell me all-day toasted waffle buffets aren't good for parrots. So I don't give Pearl a waffle very often—and he surrenders to this reality by remaining open to the other (healthier) foods I offer and not screaming too long or too loudly when he wants a toasted waffle and I don't deliver it yet again.

In this way, Pearl surrenders to life on life's terms on a daily basis—and I do my best to follow suit. For example, as a total neat freak, it is all I can do not to vacuum the feathers right off the bird when he goes into full-scale molt yet again. But I love life with Pearl, so I surrender to the rest of the terms of the deal–which includes seed hulls, dander, dust, poop, and the all-too-frequent bird-wide molts.

To us, the word "surrender" translates directly to mean "man up." Do the deal—live the life you are given AND make it a great one.

Together—"one day at a time" so to speak—we are getting it done.

Both Beautiful and Loud

As with any mother of small children, when you are a parront, you just never know what might come out of your own mouth on any given day.

Spend enough time engaged in repetitive yet soul-searching monologues about who is prettiest, where the cockatiel poop you just found on the carpet came from, and why your breakfast waffle has a head-sized hole chewed through the center of it, and the most inane things can suddenly start to seem conversation-worthy.

One day you might even find yourself saying to your feathery companion with total sincerity, "How lucky is Mommy to have a birdie who is both beautiful AND loud!" And you really, really mean it.

This is because parrots wear their minds and their hearts on their sleeves. Unlike with most of the humans I cohabitate, work, and play with, I never have to wonder what my pint-size bundle of fluff is thinking or feeling or what he wants. If he is hungry, he dives headfirst into his food bowl (or my dinner plate, whichever is closer and looks more enticing). If his neck feathers itch, he head-butts me or nibbles on my arm hairs until the only sure path back to sanity is to reprioritize my to-do list, moving "scratch neck feathers" into the topmost position. If he is tired, he will alternately nap or screech, depending on what is the best tactic for that specific situation (sudden, silent, unannounced naps are for daytime; escalating shrieks are for when it is bedtime and Mom needs to put the cage cover on and lower the lights already.)

When Pearl wants companionship, he lets me know by being sure not to stop squawking until I come to collect him. The instant I arrive at his side and pick him up, the squawking ceases. If he is bored, he will shred whatever is handy or jump onto my laptop as I type to indicate it is time to play a fun and rousing game of "relocate the cockatiel" instead of all that dull writing work. If he wants to move to a different location, he often lapses back into a display of the world's cutest chick begging behaviors, arching his back, spreading his wings slightly, opening his beak, and quivering his feathers in the direction of where he wants to go.

Watching him, sometimes I think God or Darwin or whoever it was didn't do us *Homo sapiens* any favors when they turbo-charged our prefrontal cortexes. In fact, today's animal science has proved parrots are plenty smart enough to handle complex and even abstract thought—if ever they felt the need (which mostly they don't). Rather, my parrot thinks just enough to name the issue at hand and identify an appropriate solution. Then he stops thinking and puts absolutely all the rest of his energy towards making that solution happen as fast as possible.

In the world of science this spartan and focused use of thought is called "Occam's Razor." Occam's Razor states,

All things being equal, the simplest explanation tends to be the right one.

When I watch my beautiful, loud, and intelligent parrot making daily use of Occam's Razor to solve life's challenges, what emerges day after day is pure and simple timeless wisdom:

Life = living. Hungry = eat. Lonely = connect. Bored = play. Tired = sleep.

Of course, my supersized prefrontal cortex likes to psych me out by telling me this simple approach to life might work quite well for a parrot but it certainly won't work for his parront, whose life is much more complicated.

For instance, I have to work and earn rent money, which means I have to find a job (and then keep it—a step which has at times proved particularly problematic). If I am looking for love, I have to wade through hundreds of scary online dating profiles or strange men sitting on barstools, any one of whom might be a cat owner or a serial killer. When I am hungry, I have to decide what to eat and when to eat it and how much and what if I poison myself with my own cooking? Feeling tired could mean I am ill/hung-over/depressed/oh-god-what-if....? If I discover I am bored I have to figure out what I want to do and how much it will cost and how to afford it and who to do it with or should I just go alone...?

See? MUCH more complicated, right?

But if I take a page from Pearl's book, hit the brakes on the prefrontal cortex train before it jackknifes over the mental cliff (yet again) and apply Occam's Razor instead, what I essentially get is this:

Life = living. Hungry = eat. Lonely = connect. Bored = play. Tired = sleep.

Hmmmm.

<u>Lessons with Wings:</u> *All things being equal, the simplest explanation tends to be the right one...regardless of species and for pretty much everything.*

No Biting

"Pearl! No BITING! What does Mommy mean when she says no biting? Does she mean NO biting? What did Mommy say, PEARL!"

Of course this is a rhetorical question. What I said was "no biting."

What Pearl heard was an attempt to convince him biting wasn't the perfect response to whatever his mommy had just done or not done that was out of alignment with what he wanted me to do or not do. In this way, it is not just difficult to win an argument with a parrot—it is impossible. This is because there are no arguments. There is only the parrot's perspective and whatever energy you feel like wasting by attempting to quarrel with fact.

To compound matters, parrots are very cute, which basically makes them discipline's worst nightmare. When Pearl bites, he knows it hurts. He knows he could probably have chosen another equally effective (if less satisfying) means to get his message across. But he also knows if he waits until I am done yelling and reaches out his beak again—not to bite this time but to gently nibble the end of my nose, which is the equivalent of a parrot "I'm sorry, Mom"—I will likely (100 percent) melt and instantly forgive him. If he plays his cards right with a few more oh-so-cute nose nibbles, I might even offer up a waffle treat to thank him for being so sweet.

He is, after all, such a good, good bird.

On this note, for a healthy dose of parrontal humor it doesn't get much better than *The Cockatiel Handbook* (any one of several so-named handbooks will do). The parrot discipline sections (thinly disguised under chapter titles like "Feeding" and "Understanding Cockatiel Behavior") are particularly entertaining.

The habit of allowing a tame bird to "eat at the table" should be discouraged. When you are dining, leave the bird in its cage and give it a piece of brown bread or a bit of cheese.

My first issue with this passage is not even with the word "it" (which surprises even me). It is with the word "allow."

As a parront, I don't allow biting. I also don't allow pooping on the sofa, windowsill, carpet, or my bare shoulder. Chewing grout, shredding library books, uprooting the delicate keys on my pricey laptop keyboard, and jumping into the middle of my dinner plate are all strictly off-limits. Yet each of these events happens in our household nearly every single day. In a parront's world, words like "allow" are subjective terms—used solely to make the parront feel better, and not to imply parrot comprehension (which is high) might ever lead to parrot adherence (which will always be reliably low).

As well, psychologically speaking, if I happened to be a small cute sociable flocking bird and the entire rest of my "flock" had gathered around the dinner table to talk, laugh, and consume interesting looking delicacies I might also want to try, the chances of me sitting quietly in my cage with a piece of brown bread or a bit of cheese are exactly zero percent. I would be shrieking my head off to COME GET ME ALREADY and that is exactly what my parrot does. And I don't blame him one bit.

And I also get up and get him—shrieking or no shrieking—biting or no biting—every single time.

<u>Lessons with Wings</u>: *Over the years I have learned that each parrot, like each person, has his or her own unique personality. For instance, some are more quiet and shy while others are the life of the party. But all parrots are flock animals. Their desire to be with their flock, doing whatever we are doing, is hardwired into their DNA— for survival as well as quality of life reasons. So when Pearl indicates a desire to participate in flock activities, I do my level best to find a safe and appropriate way for him to join in with us.*

I Spy Someone Pretty

Parronts be warned—this game is not for the faint of self-esteem.

I say this because, whereas we large featherless beings may at least attempt to pretend not to be checking ourselves out in every reflective surface we pass by, parrots see no need for such displays of false modesty.

This, of course, is because they do not have any modesty—false or otherwise. Modesty is for beings who are still on the fence about their own prettiness. But once you know how pretty you are, there is no reason not to (loudly, frequently) share your happy discovery with everyone else.

In the spirit of how "I Spy Someone Pretty" was always intended to be played, passing reflective surfaces offers a particularly advantageous opportunity to admire your own prettiness, perform optional small cosmetic touchups, and invite others to enjoy how pretty you are with you. For instance, let's say you are riding on somebody's shoulder and out of the corner of your round black eyes you spy that cute triangular purple mirror—the one in which you always look so pretty. So at this point it is good to start shrieking, digging in your claws, flapping your wings, and arching your neck forward to let your ride know you want to make a stop. Once you have ordered the stop, you can then let your ride know through multiple appreciative chirps, mirror feedings, and feather preenings that this will be your destination...for the foreseeable future.

From a parront's perspective, the reliable eagerness of all parrots to admire themselves in any and all reflective surfaces—no matter how cloudy, inaccessible, or off-limits the item may be—has advantages and disadvantages. On the days you conduct work conference calls from your home office, placing something reflective within eyeshot of a certain shrieking feathery someone can achieve what (literally) nothing else will—contented, extended avian silence.

However, when your formerly sweet and gentle feathered companion suddenly begins lunging in your direction, beak bared, to defend his newfound "friend in the mirror" from rivals (aka you), this is your cue to conclude that day's self-admiration session and remove the reflective thing ASAP.

Otherwise, "mirror attachment" can quickly become an all-consuming pastime (this is because, unlike *Homo sapiens*, cockatiels are not quite so quick to realize the very pretty reflection they see in the mirror is just that—a reflection.)

<u>Lessons with Wings</u>: *"Mirror attachment" is a common phenomenon with parrots, and especially with smaller members of the parrot species. Pearl, like all parrots, is a flock bird. In the wild, he would spend his days winging about with dozens or perhaps even hundreds of other cockatiels, singing, mating, raising eggs, preening, foraging, and snoozing. But in captivity, his days are spent with me...and me. It is little wonder then that he enjoys the opportunity to gaze into the eyes of a familiar face once or one hundred times a day. Since Pearl is at the mercy of his instincts, as his parront, it falls to me to manage "mirror time" so his enjoyment doesn't turn into frustration or obsession.*

77 Grams

"77 grams? 77 grams?! What happened to 75 grams??"

We are sitting in Dr. Fix's office—again. One too many unauthorized flights later, Pearl has really banged up his wing on the wall/door/floor this time and his mommy can't seem to stop the bleeding. After the usual left wing examination and application of gooey yellow styptic powder, we move on to the checks—beak check, cere check, eye check, feet check,vent check…weight check.

The weight check delivers some startling news. A certain formerly lean feathery someone now weighs in on the "heavy side of normal" for his petite weight class. As Dr. Fix runs his fingers along either side of my shrieking angel's breastbone feeling for fat deposits, his mommy begins to mentally run through the list of possible culprits—could it be the waffle treats? The extra helpings of millet? The sunflower seeds? The grilled cheese sandwiches, homemade bread, muffins, pizza? All of the above?

Whatever the cause is, Dr. Fix doesn't want to see Pearl get any rounder. And it is up to me to do that-thing-I-cannot-do and put. my. bird. on. a. diet.

For the entire first week of the new "healthy avian eating plan" (after two decades spent battling an eating disorder, "diet" is just not a word that sits comfortably in my post-recovery vocabulary) the sole reluctant participant screams. And screams. The waffles are nowhere to be found. The millet is also gone. Even the sunflower seeds are becoming scarce. In their place…kale. Spinach. Oatmeal.

A certain carb-loving gourmand with feathers is not pleased.

Two weeks into the healthy avian eating plan, Pearl's protests are finally becoming less vigorous. We decide it is time for a visit to

Grandma and Grandpa's so he can sit on the aeronautically-calibrated chef's weighing scale my mom uses to do...well I don't actually know what she normally does with it, to be honest. But today it is going to be used for an official birdie weigh-in. We get the scale out and turn it on, adjusting the setting to "grams." It is nice and round and shiny. Someone with grey and white feathers hops on to admire himself. The reading comes back...78 grams.

At this point I decide I need a vodka-tonic. And some carbs. Sometimes parronthood isn't all it is cracked up to be. Luckily, after posting about Pearl's mysterious weight fluctuations on the National Cockatiel Society Facebook page, one click leads to another and I somehow land on an article that mentions the need to weigh the avian in question at the same time each day—preferably on an empty stomach and A.P. (after pooping). The article's author explains that if one day's weight reading is taken on an empty stomach and the next day the same exact bird is weighed on a full stomach, the weight can fluctuate by as much as (wait for it) 2 to 3 grams.

Armed with this vital new intel, I decide to give the new healthy avian eating plan another week to take effect. Seven days later Pearl hops onto the cooking scale once again, and we all gather around as it swiftly delivers its verdict: "76 grams."

I feel like running victory laps around the kitchen, but we settle for the next best thing...a delicious celebratory waffle brunch, baked up fresh by Grandma for her beloved grandbird.

<u>Lessons with Wings</u>: *When I was little, I remember my mom saying, "everything in moderation." At the time I had no idea what she meant. After a two-decade fight-to-the-death with an eating disorder, I finally started to comprehend her meaning. But becoming a parront has elevated the concept of moderation to a whole new level. Not only am I charged with keeping my little guy healthy and happy, but I am caring for a member of a species that is not my own, and he is totally dependent on me to make wise choices for us both. It is not a responsibility I take lightly.*

Adventures in Chop

Indiana Jones is afraid of snakes—which is totally reasonable since snakes are very scary.

In the same way, I am afraid of parrot chop.

As a girl I automatically assumed people ate people food and parrots ate parrot food. This translated in my mind to mean I ate whatever my mom cooked and my parrots ate birdseed out of the bag the pet shop lady sold to us.

Since my mom's cooking was tasty and my parrots always seemed delighted by an offer of more birdseed, I gave it little further thought....until Mom gifted Pearl and me with a membership to the National Cockatiel Society and I met some other actual parronts. After posting one too many Facebook snapshots of a certain feathery someone chowing down on toasted waffles yet again, I was informed in no uncertain terms that pet parrots require a varied diet.

When queried for details, the NCS breeders explained how a proper parrot diet should include items other than birdseed and waffles. Pressed for further specifics, these parrot pros recommended preparing something called "parrot chop." The word "preparing" made me nervous so I asked for clarification. At this point I learned "chop" is often composed of fairly equal parts non-cooked and cooked foods all mixed together (imagine pouring your breakfast, lunch, and dinner all together into a food processor and pressing the "on" switch and you'll have a pretty good visual of the finished product).

Since the only recipe I feel confident preparing involves two slices of bread, cheese, butter, and a skillet, this was quickly adding up to more parrot-related kitchen time than I had bargained for. Not to mention that the least complicated parrot chop recipe I could find weighed in at four pages, complete with detailed instructions and an ingredients list requiring an internet connection and a dictionary app. Some of the recipes ran upwards of 15 pages and included videos, full-color photos, and even hands-on "chop workshops."

At this point I did the only reasonable thing left to do—I called Mom. She promptly produced a food processor, most of the items I didn't recognize on the ingredients list, enough enthusiasm to cancel out my participation almost completely, and repeated assurances that "of course Pearl will love the chop."

My profession is ruled by something called the *Diagnostic Standards Manual*. Currently in its fifth controversial edition, the DSM contains an entire section on eating disorders, including information about a condition called "selective eating disorder." SED happens when an individual only wants to eat certain foods—ever. While the DSM doesn't specifically mention parrots, I am sure this is just an editing oversight. Waffles, birdseed, sunflower seeds, millet, whole grain cereal, houseplants, grilled cheese sandwiches, the occasional lettuce leaf or chunk of watermelon, pizza, pasta, bread, and anything I specifically do not want him to eat remain perennially on Pearl's "approved foods list." Most everything else is contraindicated per SED, which of course includes practically every item in the average chop recipe.

To further complicate matters, in the wild parrots learn fairly early on which items are safe to eat and which are not. So introducing new unknown foods into a parrot's diet later in life basically translates as "Mom's suddenly trying to kill me." The only way around this roadblock is to personally consume the new item right in front of your parrot. In the case of parrot chop, this meant I would be signing up for an ongoing breakfast routine that included my usual beloved kefir yogurt, fresh sliced fruit, hot jasmine tea…and a heaping side dish of parrot chop.

Yum. But love for a parrot (combined with increasing peer pressure from one's fellow parronts) is a powerful force. So Mom and I powered up the food processor and went to work.

The first batch contained various greens—rendered into helpless slivers of their former selves by the wicked processor blade—mixed in with cooked oatmeal, couscous, quinoa, flax seeds, red lentils, various spices, and mung bean sprouts. I dropped a small mound into Pearl's bowl, garnishing it with millet and whole grain cereal plus a few token sunflower seeds as "bait." Then I waited. The diner drew near. Nearer. Nearer…he dipped his small white and grey feathery head trustingly down into the bowl…opened his beak…then quickly reared his head back and gave me an accusatory look that clearly asked, "Mom, why are you suddenly trying to kill me?!?"

This went on for the prescribed two-hours-long morning chop offering period. The moment it was over I rewarded him with a waffle for effort. He ate heartily. The next day we tried again. This time, in a surprising twist, Pearl approached my breakfast bowl and actually ingested minute portions of my freshly sliced fruit—the better to avoid the chop in his own bowl, of course. I rewarded him with part of my blueberry pancake. He thoroughly enjoyed all of the portions that contained no nutrient-rich blueberries.

To date, our morning chop-and-avoid routine remains intact. But I continue trying because that is what conscientious parronts do.

And Pearl continues taking the long way around his breakfast bowl…for now.

<u>Lessons with Wings</u>: *Given my personal eating disorders history, confronting the need to change my 12-year-old parrot's diet has been one of the more challenging parront-related tasks I've tackled. After worrying that a) he would starve, b) his seemingly intractable seed preferences would lead to fatty liver disease or worse, c) I would get hauled off to parront jail by the chop police, or d) all of the above, I have finally begun to calm down. In the same way I cannot reverse any damage my earlier eating disordered habits may have caused to my own body, with Pearl all I can do is forge ahead, armed with my newfound knowledge, and give him the option to enjoy a nutritionally sound future.*

Extra Yucky

When you are a parront, you soon learn helpful techniques to categorize daily events.

For instance, there are events that are just "yucky." An example might be walking across the room barefoot and feeling dried cockatiel poop embedded into the weave of your hideous brown living room carpet.

Other events might be considered "yuckier." For instance, perhaps you are about to sit down and you discover cockatiel poop encrusted onto the back of your favorite wrought iron bird-themed kitchen chair.

Some events, however, can only be properly categorized as "extra yucky." For instance, let's say you are wearing shorts while sitting in your favorite wrought iron bird-themed kitchen chair with your parrot snoozing on your bare thigh. All of a sudden, you see your bird shake himself awake, squat, and right after that something very warm and wet begins to ooze down your leg.

"Extra yucky"—no questions asked.

Sometimes I look down at the end of a long day of writing and notice the small garbage can beside my desk is literally filled with white paper towels. Each paper towel has played its own essential role in removing occurrences of yucky, yuckier, and extra yucky from my hair/leg/chair back/carpet/laptop keyboard. As I gaze at this crumpled white pile, two things occur. One, I feel infinitely grateful to (and more than a little in love with) that brilliant soul who invented the "paper towel." And two, I realize that, after counting up the number of daily squats that towering white pile represents, my avian's tiny thigh muscles are likely vastly stronger than my own.

This is probably the right time to mention that finicky neat-nick types of people and parrots tend to be incompatible. Unfortunately, I am a finicky neat-nick type of person, which means running out of wine or Cheetos® or even dark chocolate might not prompt a midnight run to the supermarket, but ripping the very last paper towel off of its little cardboard roll certainly will. Here, whenever possible, I also prefer to use the "select-a-size" paper towels to more accurately customize the amount of paper towel I rip off to the appropriate category of daily event I am attempting to wipe up.

No need to waste all of that perfectly good, strong, thick paper towel on a category "yucky" when an "extra yucky" is sure to follow…soon.

<u>Lessons with Wings</u>: *There is a thin line separating "finicky neat-nick" and "obsessively compulsive clean freak"—at least in my world. What this means is that, each and every day, I wake up to yet another mandatory day-long session of parrot-centric "neat-nick therapy" as feathers, dander, seed hulls, poop, and other avian-related detritus begins to cover my spotless floors, chairs, sofa, and pillows once again. There is little doubt in my mind my home would be cleaner without Pearl in it. But without Pearl, I also wouldn't want to live there.*

Just Add Sound

Technically, "miming" is supposed to be an act performed without sound. But some mimes like to add in sound—lots of sound.

Especially if there is an urgent message to transmit and the audience doesn't seem to be receiving it (or receiving it fast enough) combining physical movement with helpful sound cues can speed up both delivery and response.

For example, let's say the mime in question is hungry. But the waffle is currently situated in an unfavorable location. Addressing this with movement alone, such as arching the body and head forward, extending the wings, pointing the crest feathers, and widening the eyes may be sufficient to accomplish delivery under ordinary conditions. However, if the mime's large featherless assistant has become inattentive for some reason (because she is eating the mime's waffle, for instance) boosting the message with sound can refocus the assistant's attention and re-emphasize the need for a prompt and favorable response.

In the same way, when sound alone is employed, communications may lack sufficient clarity. For instance, frequently humans get confused because what one person says and what the other person hears are two different things. So perhaps my mom might say to my dad, "Paul, don't you think it would be fun to bake this bread together?" Here, my dad could be forgiven for assuming this is an open-ended question with multiple answer options. However, if he replies, "No, Dana, that doesn't sound like fun to me," he will soon learn the question wasn't open-ended after all.

It is even easier to see this with the non-human members of the household. Sometimes my folks will decide their continually snoozing dachshund, J.P. Morgan, needs to get some exercise. So they will look right at Morgan and say, "Morgan, come!" They think the instruction is perfectly clear. But Morgan might hear "come right now," "come later on," or even (and most likely) "come only if and/or when you feel like it."

This is where miming out the desired action while adding sound can be the perfect resolution for lapses in both intra- and interspecies communications. For instance, when you want to be taken to the large reflective surface in the bathroom so you can admire your feathers, spreading out your wings, hanging off the end of your assistant's finger or shoulder in the general direction of the bathroom door, opening your beak, clenching your claws, and issuing a series of escalating shrieks gets the communication off to the best possible start. Next, shrieking louder while flapping vigorously (when your assistant moves further away from the bathroom door) and shifting to soft appreciative chirps with only semi-extended wings (when your assistant moves closer to the bathroom door) will deliver crystal-clear micro course-corrections where necessary.

Perhaps most importantly, communicating via mimed movements while adding sound ensures both auditory and visual learners will receive (and act upon) the message with the utmost speed and accuracy.

<u>Lessons with Wings</u>: *One of many things Pearl has taught me is that parrots are "extreme communicators." In the wild, every chirp, every shriek, every head dip, every shrug is a message. In the not-so-wild, the instinct for unceasing communication remains. No message is too unimportant to be transmitted. "Mom, I ate all my millet please bring more." "Mom, I'm going to nap now." "Mom, I'm awake from my nap." "Mom, don't I look pretty?" "Mom, I'm bored." "Mom, this is the best ladder ever." The point of the communication may not be any point at all beyond "to communicate." I feel so lucky I get to share my life with a companion who wants to share each and every moment of his life with me, shriek by shriek by shriek.*

When the Time Comes

Sometimes I tell myself Pearl will live forever. This makes me very, very happy. But I know it isn't true.

Then I tell myself that this time, when it is my avian's time to go, I will be so advanced in my meditation practice I will simply breathe him softly into the great Void via my placid Buddha-nature. Luckily, Pearl will only need to survive for about 800 more years so I can work up to this goal.

The truth is, I hit an absolutely amazing, immeasurable level of wimpy-ness when my pets die. Whenever this happens, pet-less people who know me sometimes inquire, "How old are you again?" I always tell them, "Five." Some days I feel 80, and when people ask me my age on these days I might say "80." But on the days my pets die I feel five—so unendingly sad, so utterly disbelieving, so irrevocably stuck in a rut of denial where all I want to do is stomp my not-so-little-anymore feet and yell, "It's NOT FAIR!!!" So I do. I do it until my steadfast, absolutely unyielding denial gives way to anger, to bargaining, to sadness, and at last to begrudging acceptance. I know I have reached the "acceptance" stage of the grief process when I come home with a new pet.

At which point the process starts all over again.

I have had pets—birds, mostly, along with some turtles and fish and dogs and I think gerbils once—since I was eight years old. In so doing, I have tried every which way I can to avoid the issue of pet death. I will probably keep trying until, well, you know. Yet to date it seems like having a pet, in the same way as having a child, a mate, a best friend, parents, or other "emotional belongings," just comes with both love and loss inevitably attached. They are each just part of the package. We don't get to customize the package. We don't get to say, "Yes I want the love part and the life part but not the grief part and the death part—so don't charge me for those okay."

So while I would like to envision how calm, stoic, poised, and peaceful I will be when the time finally draws near for Pearl to pass, there is no sense wasting precious energy and common sense imagining anything of the sort.

Because when the time comes, I will be five all over again.

<u>Lessons with Wings</u>: *Grief happens. It has happened to me many times before, and it will happen to me many times again. Denial. Anger. Bargaining. Sadness. Acceptance. These are the stages of grief. Is loving Pearl every day of our life together worth the price of the inevitable grief yet to come? Absolutely.*

The Littlest Pterodactyl

I'll just go ahead and say it.

Dinosaurs. Are. Cool.

As proof (on the off chance you actually need any) I submit for your inspection the following.

Exhibit A: Two nephews, ages six and two, who are even now industriously exchanging their parents' cash for a museum-worthy assortment of all things prehistoric. The current pooled collection includes pajamas, t-shirts, backpacks, digging kits, 3-D goggles, picture books, mechanized action figures with moveable limbs and real roars, glow-in-the-dark wall art, and of course underwear and/or diapers (depending on which nephew you are and how well potty training is going that particular week).

Exhibit B: One writer-auntie, age 42, who regularly attends her local natural science museum's annual Halloween extravaganza featuring several hundred incognito adult revelers and one exact to-scale skeletal replica of *T. rex*.

Halloween just isn't Halloween without *T. rex*.

But since much of the dinosaurs' enduring allure centers around the whole sucks-to-be-you giant comet extinction issue, the question on the table today then becomes: if the dinosaurs had survived the Ice Age, would we still find them so fascinating?

Since I just so happen to cohabitate with one of their many tiny descendants, I can help with this: "Yup." In fact, the way I see it, the dinosaurs of our generation are cooler than ever. For starters, modern dinosaurs are fun-size and feathery. Add to this that today's dinosaurs prove you don't have to be fanged to be fierce (as an example: macaw beaks can supposedly crush up to 700 pounds of weight per square inch—think voracious slobbering Doberman attached to your leg and you'll have a fairly accurate visual.)

Best of all, today's dinosaurs have groovy ancestors. For instance, paleontologists recently unearthed what they like to call *Pegomastax africanus* and I like to call the vulture-headed, parrot-beaked, cat-bodied, porcupine-quilled mini-dinosaur. As well, archeologists and others skilled in such things can now definitively link today's diminutive grey tufted Titmouse to the giant Velociraptor, common garden chickens to none other than *T. rex*, and Archaeopteryx (aka the "First Bird") to, well, pretty much everything else with feathers.

Or, as *Birdology* author Sy Montgomery writes:

...birds are living dinosaurs. To the nimble likes of predatory Velociraptors, birds owe their speed and their smarts. To dinosaurs, they owe their otherworldly appeal—and as well, surely, some of their transcendent mystery and beauty. For this is one of the great miracles of birds, greater, perhaps, than that of flight: when the chickens in my backyard come to my call, or when I look into the sparkling eye of a chickadee, we are communing across a gap of more than 300 million years.

<u>Lessons with Wings</u>: *When some people look at a book, they just see a book. As a writer and avid reader, when I look at a book I see the author's story, the book's story, interesting cover art, an opportunity to learn, and so much more. In the same way, when some people look at a bird, they just see a bird. When I look at a bird, I see millions of years' worth of fascinating history and a bird. A very cute bird. A very very cute bird. A very very very cute...*

Mommy's Little Helper

There is a reason why many young couples that aspire to have children start out with a dog. A parrot can be an equally good choice for exactly the same reason.

For instance, let's just say you have a number of must-do items on today's to-do list. Now imagine you have an enthusiastic yet unskilled sidekick (with wings) who insists on "helping" with every. single. item. on. your. list.

This is precisely why I have gotten so good at calculating how long certain routine tasks like laundry, meals, sweeping, and writing assignments will take under two sets of circumstances: "with bird" and "without bird." I have found that by adding between one and 24 hours to each "with bird" task I can get a reasonably accurate assessment of how long each item on that day's to-do list will take to complete if the feathered member of our household participates.

Yet if I have time, "with bird" is always my preferred option. Reason being—left to my own devices I might feel less than pumped about yet another session of vacuuming (feathers, dander, poop, seed hulls, et al) off the living room carpet. But add in a tiny hookbill who greets the vacuum cleaner like a long-lost BFF and suddenly I'm transformed into Snow White's eighth cheerful whistling dwarf.

Another particularly wonderful side effect of having to adapt nearly everything I do to include a "with bird" option is that I must then be realistic about what I can hope to accomplish in any given day. Take cleaning, for instance. Do I really need to clean the entire house right now—or can certain rooms wait a little longer so Pearl and I can cut up the fresh breakfast strawberries together? (For the record, my part of this particular task is the washing, slicing, dicing, and storing. Pearl's part is to grab the green leafy tops, drag them across the counter in a red, streaky, slightly creepy-looking single-file line, and then nibble on them, leaving tiny green leafy confetti behind for "us" to clean up.)

However, there are some tasks where "without bird" is the only viable option. Examples include anything that involves using cleaning supplies, exiting to the outside of the house, turning on the stove or oven, or climbing ladders. Here the feathery member of the Household Task Force Completion Team is likely to protest his necessary exclusion both loudly and ceaselessly. Because of this, I have often found it helpful to clump these tasks together into one group I can do all at once, and then line up an alternate activity for Pearl to enjoy while I'm working.

Since it isn't nearly as much fun to do "without bird" tasks, this is also a near-guarantee I will complete those tasks as fast as possible to leave more time for "with bird" activities later.

Lessons with Wings: *While Mommy's little helper may not be as speedy or adept as I am at certain practical tasks on my daily to-do list, my feathered bundle of joy brings other essential gifts to the table—specifically, the shared companionship, laughter, and love that makes any of it worth doing in the first place.*

Mornings

If you happen to be born with wings and feathers, other beings tend to automatically assume you also like to wake up early.

Not in our household.

This morning my alarm went off at 4:45 a.m. I was catching an "early bird" flight to speak at a university, which meant someone feathery would also have to get up so I could refresh his food and water and get him all situated for comfort during the brief time I would be away.

At 4:50am I turned on the bedside lamp and began our usual wakeup ritual, crooning, "Where is the prettiest bird in the whole world? Where *iiiiis* he?? Where is Mommy's beautiful birdie???" I flipped back his light blue cage cover—aware as I did so of the sound of vicious hissing. The hissing continued as I unlatched his cage door and swung it open. I then extended my finger into his cage, placed it under his breastbone, and was rewarded with a hearty bite.

Eventually I managed to extract my grumpy avian from his cage so I could replace his cage-bottom paper. He perked up for a few minutes when I whistled to him. But the moment I turned my back he scrambled right back into his cage and up onto his favorite sleeping perch. I caught him in the act of tucking his head under his wing and turned on the overhead light full force. He hissed and glared.

To be fair, I felt exactly the same way. If I had had anyone to hiss at—or to bite for that matter—I would have happily indulged. No being should have to wake up at 4:45 a.m., a time of day when even the noisy nesting sparrows in my eaves are still blissfully snoozing. If the sky is still dark, clearly it is not yet time to start one's day (a cherished personal belief which two full decades' worth of former employers have been unable to successfully dislodge).

But being currently out of other options, I stretched, showered, chose an outfit, fixed my hair, attempted to administer an abbreviated version of parrot breakfast, printed my boarding passes, and manhandled my luggage out the door—supervised all the while by a miniature yet menacing grey falcon. The moment I dimmed the lights and returned him to his sleeping perch, Pearl promptly snapped both eyes shut and feigned sleep, clearly intent on proving once and for all that there are no "early birds" in our household.

For the record, I wholeheartedly concur.

<u>Lessons with Wings</u>: *We live in a world with so many labels; from "early bird" to "night owl," "Ivy League" to "dropout," "fat" to "skinny," "white" to "black," "young" to "old." Labels (both so-called flattering and not so flattering) are everywhere. It has taken me years to realize that labels don't have to matter. They don't have to define me—not one little bit—not unless I allow it. And when I forget this, I have a small feathered sleepyhead who is always standing at the ready to remind me!*

Sufficiency

I'm not much of a faith scholar, but there is one particular Bible verse that never fails to intrigue me.

It talks about how we shouldn't worry about getting our needs met because God provides for the "birds of the air" —even though they apparently don't lift a claw to provide for themselves (or at least that is how it reads to me). It also seems to suggest people hold greater value to God than parrots.

This last part always makes me wonder what kind of pet God has— obviously not a parrot.

Still, the word "sufficiency" didn't enter my awareness (or wind up paper-clipped to my wall) until a mentor recommended a book called *The Soul of Money* by Lynne Twist. Not being particularly money-minded myself, I tend to struggle to feel confident about having my daily–monthly–yearly–lifetime financial needs met. So I sought out Twist's book and eagerly began to read it.

Right away I encountered two words: "scarcity" and "sufficiency." Scarcity = the awareness of "not enough." Sufficiency = the awareness of "enough." It didn't take me long to figure out which awareness I have and which awareness Pearl has. I am constantly struggling against worry about scarcity. Meanwhile, Pearl wakes up each and every day to another wonderful day of sufficiency. When he is hungry, a great variety and quantity of food near-magically appears in his bowl. When he is thirsty, he rappels down the cage bars towards the green water bottle where delicious fresh spring water always awaits.

If he gets bored, all he has to do is look around to select a nearby item to chew or dismantle. One loud shriek (or, worst case scenario, a series of loud shrieks) reliably delivers prompt companionship. When he feels sleepy, he simply locates one of his many comfortable perches, rests his head behind the softest imaginable downy wing, and enjoys yet another restful nap. His every need is met—time and time and time again—and all he has to do to experience another day of total sufficiency is to wake up into it.

While this all appears to be par for the course in my parrot's world, I have to admit I continue to find the whole thing rather extraordinary.

Aaaaargh

I would never make it as a pirate.

For starters, I hate conflict. As for carrying around a long pointed metal object in my sash, well, that's just an accident waiting to happen. Also, I don't do eye patches or bandanas—they don't work with my face shape. If I needed any more proof, sailing makes me seasick and I'm a vegetarian. Finally, bathing is not a personal grooming task I think can wait until the ship gets back to port.

Yet—oddly—pirates and I do have one lifestyle preference in common. When it comes to choosing an animal sidekick, we both pick parrots whenever possible. If all it took to become a pirate was the ability to perform nearly any task with a diminutive winged hookbill clinging to your flowing shirtsleeves, I'd be a first draft pick. I often (well not often, but occasionally) think that if I ever did get captured by pirates, I could convince them to spare my life by offering to manage the ship's aviary. I imagine in my mind this would be a lot like working as a babysitter, except with screaming parrots instead of screaming two-year-olds.

I also find it intriguing that the words "parrot" and "pirate" look and sound almost identical. For my writing business, I recently wrote an article about Parrot Cay, a private island in the Caribbean. While researching I learned this particular island happens to be a place where many celebrities like to keep vacation homes (this on account of the fact that only the richest of folks can afford to get there, let alone stay). Even more interesting, the original name of this island was apparently "Pirate Cay," but the locals changed it so as not to scare off the celebrities and their loaded visitors. From a pirate's perspective, I can't help but assume the author of this rebranding gem was instantly promoted. Why deal with the leaky boat, the grumpy prisoners, that hideous plank business, when you can be a land-bound pirate instead? It just makes logistical sense—especially if in the process you score stable housing that doesn't sink, plenty of clean water to bathe in, and your victims come sailing right up to you while you sip citrusy scurvy-repelling margaritas on a sunny beach.

From the parrot's perspective as well, shifting the whole enterprise to land solves a number of otherwise challenging conundrums. For instance, no more worrying the big tasty wooden play toy you just chewed a hole in will then sink you to the bottom of the ocean. No exhausting time-sucks as you are forced to compete again and again with the neighboring pirate ship's parrot flock for who can shriek the loudest or execute the most complex aerial display. And no risk that your parront (and you) will kick the bucket thanks to the bigger, stronger pirate bully and his bigger, stronger winged sidekick from one cove over.

That aside, I have several 40-something friends who still spend all year planning for the next annual "Talk Like a Pirate Day." On this joyful occasion, they look forward to once again donning their plastic eye patches and spending the evening yelling "Aaaargh!" at the other pretend-pirates parked on neighboring barstools.

While they are otherwise engaged, you will find me where I always am during this dubious holiday—drinking all their rum and practicing my parronting skills.

<u>Lessons with Wings</u>: *I have lots of preferences. For instance, I prefer central air conditioning to windows units, summer to winter, and classical to county music. And I prefer parrots to—well, practically everything else. I may frequently get the other choices I make wrong and have to go back and course-correct. But I've been making the choice to share my life with parrots perfectly since I was eight years old and I have no plans to stop now!*

Crunchy Versus Puffy

Recently Target started selling "small grab" size bags of Cheetos® at the checkout registers.

I seldom let myself buy "big grab" bags of Cheetos® because, well, if one Cheeto tastes delicious, 100 Cheetos® will probably be even tastier. With the invention and launch of the "small grab," however, this delicate issue has been somewhat alleviated.

Unlike his mommy, my avian is not constrained by this sort of number, um, crunching. Plus, frankly, there is more to love about Cheetos® than just their cheesy synthetic orange goodness. When you're a parrot, it would be a pure waste of perfectly good free entertainment to overlook the shiny allure of that small avian-sized body bag the chips are packaged in. While Pearl loathes those expensive yellow "bird snuggly" toys parronts can buy (they are like a birdie-sized sleeping bag, for lack of a better description) and he won't go anywhere near one, the moment he sees the brightly colored Cheetos® bag with its glistening oily silver interior, he marches right in.

And I do mean IN.

The first time it happened, I was typing away on my laptop, absentmindedly nabbing a Cheeto from the bag every now and again. The rustling sound caught the attention of a certain feathery someone, and out of the corner of my eye I noticed him inching closer to investigate. The next time I looked up, all I saw was a tail. The rest of his approximately seven-inch bird body had disappeared completely into the interior of the bag. I did what any concerned parront would do at that point. I started snapping pictures and posting them on Facebook.

It just so happened I had chosen a bag of crunchy Cheetos® for my afternoon snack that day. So the next day, I decided it would be both fun and scientifically educational to conduct a taste test.

To begin, I invited a sole randomly selected, certified objective panelist (with feathers) to participate. Next, I picked out a bag of puffy Cheetos®—my personal favorite. To set up the test, I first loudly opened the bag. Then I placed it in the exact same position beside my laptop. From there, I adopted the identical casual demeanor from the day before, typing away while occasionally swiping a puffy Cheeto from the bag to snack on. Once again, the rustling sound of the bag wafted by a keen set of avian ears. This time apparently it sounded both familiar and welcome, because the participant was observed to run, not walk, towards the open edges of the bag. Then, in the exact same manner as was observed the prior day, he dove in face-first.

While I didn't use a stopwatch, it appeared the participant spent approximately the same amount of time pulverizing the contents of both the crunchy and puffy Cheetos® bags. When he emerged, I would say (qualitatively speaking of course) he had approximately the same quantity of tiny orange pieces adhering to the outside edges of his beak (and neck, and chest, and crest feathers). And he certainly seemed equally delighted with the overall construction, color scheme, and interior design of each bag.

In which case, and doing the best I can to correctly interpret the extremely unsubtle enthusiasm our participant displayed for each independently administered, unsolicited bag of test product, it would appear the Cheetos® "crunchy versus puffy" taste test results delivered an even tie.

<u>Lessons with Wings</u>: *Parronts should never feed their parrots Cheetos®. Frankly, parronts should never feed themselves Cheetos®. Yet in this age of ever higher-tech toys (for humans and avians alike) I can't help but find it beyond charming that Pearl and I can spend a full afternoon together, happily entertained with nothing more than 99 cents and a shiny silver bag between us.*

The One with the Feathers is My Favorite

I am flattened on the couch. My ears are blocked. My nose…isn't. Niagara Falls has inexplicably relocated to my throat in the middle of the night.

Each shriek, chirp, and whistle emanating from a certain feathery someone's nearby cage streaks through my head like a sniper's bullet, intent on picking off individual brain cells one by one, just for fun.

I look over at Pearl, training one bleary eye on him. "Pearl, baby, can you please just…not…" He utters a happy chirp, thrilled to feel his mommy's watchful eye meet his. He chirps again—cocking his head at that impossibly cute angle that has given him a rabid Facebook fan following and an increasingly sizeable chunk of my remaining iCloud storage space. I sigh. Haul my aching body off the sofa. Snap a few more photos as he poses. And poses. And poses.

Ignoring the threat of yet another snot bomb set to deploy at any moment from my left nostril, I place one gentle kiss and then another and another on top of my bird's soft downy head. "The one with the feathers is my favorite," I croon. Pearl cheeps happily again. Another brain cell bites the dust.

I remember once when I was in the middle of production for my first music CD. My producer came down with the flu, which he then generously shared with his wife. One day after they were on the mend I arrived as usual for my session. His wife popped in to say hello and I asked them both how they were feeling. She replied, "It was awful. We were sooooo so SO so sick. I don't think either of us have ever been that sick in our entire lives. The only good thing about it was that we could at least share it together."

At the time I remember thinking to myself, "One of us is certifiable and I'm pretty sure it isn't me." But today, peering dizzily up at the winged member of our household while simultaneously sneezing and honking into a mangled tissue, I knew exactly how she felt. There are worse things than conducting germ warfare accompanied by one's absolute favorite life form.

Infinitely worse things.

<u>Lessons with Wings</u>: *Life is full of curve balls. I used to experience this with negativity, so aware of and comfortable inside the darkness I would run after it when it tried to leave. But today I have a small fluffy mentor who teaches me that the presence of darkness offers a great reminder to look for light. And since light seems to follow Pearl wherever he goes, my plan from here forward is simply this—to stay as close to Pearl as possible.*

Seeing Green

More than one animal species is known to exhibit color fixation.

A classic example is the herring gull. Soon after birth, hungry chicks instinctively begin to lunge for the bright red dot on the underside of their parents' bills (this triggers Mom or Dad to vomit up the chicks' favorite supper—still-digesting fish). Gulls aren't alone in their reaction to red. Chickens attack when flock mates begin to bleed. Monkeys become agitated. Bulls charge. Fish (well, the spiny stickleback anyway) start feeling amorous. And humans already know all about the power of the little red dress.

But red does nothing for Pearl. Nope. In our household, it is all about the green.

It took the sacrifice of an innocent houseplant to alert me to my winged sidekick's primal color preferences. The truth is, I used to have a bit of a houseplant problem. I would go to the grocery store and casually wheel by the floral department as houseplant after houseplant jumped into my cart. Big ones, small ones, tall and short ones, wide and narrow ones with lovely light variegated and deep dark forest green leaves...I had houseplants in the kitchen, houseplants in the bathroom, houseplants in the living room, houseplants on the porch.

What I didn't know was, in my passion to reforest the world one efficiency apartment at a time, I might as well have been waving a bright green challenge flag in front of my eager avian's eyes. One fateful day I left Pearl unattended in the kitchen for a rare moment. When I returned, my glossy green countertop houseplant was a shadow of its former self...and Pearl was sporting what appeared to be deep green lipstick rimming the outer edges of his curved beak.

Luckily, the clearly delicious leaves were non-toxic. But from that point forward, I crossed "more houseplants" off the weekly shopping list in favor of "leafy greens." We started with spinach—reason being that spinach leaves most closely resembled those of the prior week's potted delicacy. Pearl displayed mild interest, clearly more intent on shredding than ingesting. We then moved on to broccoli. While the florets fascinated him, like certain aged cheeses the odor and strong flavor put broccoli firmly on the bench.

Next we tried kale. Or rather, I tried kale while Pearl tried the wicker basket next to my weary kale-holding fingers. At that point my spring travels were starting up again, so I dropped Pearl off for a staycation his grandparents' house. As the sole flock-wide foodie, my mom is forever attempting to expand our palates. Whoever crosses her path is fair game and Pearl is no exception. When I arrived, Mom was in the kitchen assembling a gourmet salad. As preparations commenced, she casually inquired, "Do you think Pearl would like arugula?" While I was flattered she thought I knew what "arugula" was, the easiest answer still seemed to be, "Nope."

As usual (and once again to her credit) she ignored me. When I returned from my trip, I was presented with a large Ziploc bag full of arugula labeled "For Pearl." The bag was accompanied by detailed verbal instructions for daily feedings.

To date, I continue to offer regularly scheduled single servings of arugula and other healthy greens to my feathery foodie-in-the-making. I am also happy to report our newly inaugurated "houseplant preservation project" is off to an equally successful start.

<u>Lessons with Wings</u>: *I have always loved the color blue. In the same way, Pearl loves the color green. Perhaps there is an evolutionary reason for this. Or maybe green just looks prettier than all the other colors to his UV-enhanced eyes. I don't know—in the same way I don't know why I prefer blue. What I do know is that, until just recently, I didn't know Pearl had a favorite color. This newfound knowledge—and the promise of even more yet to come—just makes our connection that much more precious to me.*

Me and Mark Bittner

In my first job out of college, I worked in the marketing department for a blue chip oil company.

This was an atrocious choice for a number of reasons, and within a few scant months of my start date it became all too clear I was allergic to the hours, the clients, my colleagues, my bosses, and the work itself. Even worse, the allergy seemed mutual.

The sole shining benefit of the position was that my assigned territory allowed me to live within driving distance of beautiful San Francisco. While making my rounds, occasionally I would hear rumors of a flock of wild parrots living near the city's famed Telegraph Hill. However, I never saw the parrots with my own eyes and for some reason I didn't ever follow up. Perhaps this was because I was already quite busy attempting to flee my job and that activity took up a lot of my time.

Luckily, Mark Bittner, the author of *The Wild Parrots of Telegraph Hill*, didn't have this problem when he first met the flock. This was because, technically, he didn't have a job when their paths first crossed...or for some time thereafter. So he had a lot more freedom to hang out with the parrots and chronicle their comings and goings.

When I started reading *The Wild Parrots of Telegraph Hill*, years after I had left both the oil company and the San Francisco area, I absolutely expected to enjoy a story about a flock of wild parrots living in close company with a fellow parrot-loving human. But I didn't foresee the added bonus of encountering an inspiring mentor in the author himself. Interestingly, Mark, like me, started out with aspirations to pursue music professionally. Like me, at some point he realized neither his lifestyle preferences nor his temperament particularly favored that career choice. At this juncture, Mark—again like me—began to drift, grieving a bit and also uncertain of where his path would lead post-music. And, like me, he eventually began to perceive in his loss of career direction an opportunity to seek deeper meaning in his life through embarking on a spiritual quest.

As time passed and our stories continued, we both found new insight and inspiration through choosing to share our lives with that most resourceful, resilient, intelligent, and sociable of companions— the parrot. We both took the demise of our musical career goals as a sign the time had finally come and we were ready to allow our questions rather than our answers to lead us forward. In the interests of this quest, we both willingly endured many years of turmoil and uncertainty, years which I often feel I am still in the midst of, but from which Mark appears to have successfully emerged, at last realizing his three deepest hopes (which also mirror my own): to meet his mate, do work he loves, and live in a beautiful place.

Perhaps *Love & Feathers* is my attempt to follow in my mentor's footsteps, ever hopeful that as I set down Pearl's and my story on paper, the mysteries of the inner shared story we are still living out together will become more tangible, meaningful, and instructive as well.

We shall see, we shall see.

You can visit Mark and his Wild Parrots anytime at:
www.markbittner.net

Lessons with Wings: *When I was younger, I used to marvel at people who seemed so at ease in the company of their own species. I still do. While it has always felt like "coming home" to be surrounded by one or many sets of soft feathered wings, navigating the complexities of human-to-human relationships has often proved more challenging. Since reading* The Wild Parrots of Telegraph Hill *I have gone on to devour countless similar stories about people and their animal companions—stories that affirm the essential connection that exists between humans and non-humans—stories of hope, love, new beginnings, ageless wisdom, and mutual salvation.*

Follow the Wings

In theory, "Follow the Wings" is a lot like the popular children's game "Follow the Leader"—except for a few noticeable departures.

For instance, in the "Leader" version, traditionally the one who gets to play the leader rotates. No such luck in the "Wings" version. Each follower, once drafted, will be expected to accept their lifetime assigned role and love it. Also, with "Leader," the leader and followers tend to be around the same size and shape. This is good for PR, in that it makes the leader look less sadistic should he, say, decide to run behind the sofa or jump onto a window ledge.

In terms of leader-led activities such as singing, human leaders (thankfully) can usually be counted on to tire after several spirited renditions of musical mimicry. Not so when the lead "singer" quite literally chirps for a living. If five echoed rounds of feathery wolf whistles are good for the leader's self-esteem, just think how good 500 rounds will feel. Looking on the bright side, however, followers will no longer need their daily jog to develop lung capacity and breath control...not to mention patience and endurance.

While the discipline may be strict, conscripted "Follow the Wing-ers" do get certain perks. In terms of maintaining optimal mental health, for example, scientists now know that regularly engaging in novel activities helps build new neural connections in the brain—no matter how old that brain or its owner happens to be. Because "Follow the Wings" is a game that can begin at any moment, follows no pre-set pattern, and may continue for any length of time, followers and their neural connections must always be ready to bring their A-game. In the realm of finances, too, who needs an expensive "smart" television or pricey concert tickets when free rounds of flock-wide karaoke are always available?

Perhaps most poignantly, however, it is hard to argue with a leader who picks you to be on their team. Speaking as a willing lifetime Wing-er myself, I can share that when I was in school, no classmate in their right mind would have selected me to be on any team of any kind—especially for activities which involved any amount of focus, aptitude, coordination, sportsmanship, interest, or comprehension of basic game rules. You throw, hit, or kick something in my direction; I'm going to either duck or run. And anyone who has ever seen me throw, hit, or kick anything in their direction has never asked me to do it twice.

Plus, I like playing "Follow the Wings." It gives me much-needed breaks from overly grown-up activities like paying bills, cranking out copy-for-pay, cleaning bird poop off the carpet, and attempting to eat fewer Cheetos®. I am not particularly good at any of these things, but as a new day dawns, my Leader is always standing by yet again to pick me as his preferred wing-woman.

And this, just like a feathery wolf whistle headed back in my direction for 499th time, quite simply feels good.

Lessons with Wings: *As a wise friend once said to me, "If you're not able to find a way to have any fun doing what you're doing, why keep doing it?" These words have become a benchmark by which I evaluate the life choices I make to this day. And if I should ever forget this lesson, I can always count on a certain feathery and fun-loving mentor to remind me!*

Role Reversal

As I type, my parents' dachshund, J.P. Morgan, is curled up in his dog bed, tuckered out from another long day of resting at our family's rental home on Cape Cod.

My mom is thumbing through the *Cape Codder*, a local paper announcing upcoming happenings (she just read me a blurb about the November Turnip Festival. Sadly, we won't be here in November). My dad is wandering around the house, weighing out loud to himself the relative merits of taking out the trash tonight in the dark or tomorrow when the sun comes back up.

Blink and you will miss it around here. Which is precisely why I like it.

Two years ago, the big excitement occurred when, after being measured tip to tail at a staggering 41 inches, Morgan once again leveled the competition at Doxie Day's "Longest Dachshund" contest. Cape gossip indicates other dachshund owners may still be feeling a bit bitter about his third consecutive win, but Dad says this is like insisting Michael Phelps shouldn't swim in the Olympics anymore because he is just too good. I have to admit Dad has a point.

This also perfectly illustrates why I often choose to spend my vacation time in a place where the ratio of human beings to everything else makes me feel like a blissfully endangered species. In my teeming home city of several million people, an experience like this is exceedingly hard to come by. But when I arrive at a place like the Cape, in the sudden and stark absence of urban humanity what I am left with is....

Clean air. Nature. The roaring surf. Sunrise. Sunset. Birds. Birds. Birds. Birds. Birds.

Did I mention birds?

The truth is, it takes an expensive plane ticket, a grueling three-hour car ride (complete with leaping deer obstacle course) and a concerted effort to set aside annual time and savings for me to reconnect with what is, for Pearl, his accepted experience of life's daily simplicity. For instance, each morning Pearl wakes up. He eats breakfast and drinks some spring water. He chirps. He preens his feathers. He admires himself in the mirror...mirrors. He shreds things. He samples new delicacies (authorized and unauthorized). He naps. He naps some more. He eats dinner. He enjoys having his neck feathers scratched. He goes to sleep, head tucked restfully behind one soft grey wing.

He is not on vacation. He does not have to carve out time to be with himself, to enjoy the loveliness of the day or the deliciousness of the off-limits houseplant he has just dismantled. Every meal is a chance to extract the goodness out of each seed and then joyfully fling the hulls just to see how far their trajectory will take them (which I can report is surprisingly far). Every nap is an opportunity to rest up for the next exciting adventure. Every shower just makes him that much prettier. Every vet visit is an event quickly forgotten—typically at the first sight of something (or someone) he adores. His enthusiasm for each moment, his alertness to every possibility, is something I wait all year long to "go on vacation" to experience.

Meanwhile, I find it alternately irritating or miraculous (depending on when you ask and what Pearl has been up to while you were asking) that the animal companions I have in the past tended to label as "less intelligent" or "dependent" are having a much better time on a daily basis than I am—simply by living their lives, trusting each moment will bring them what they need, moment by moment by moment.

In this, yet again I find our roles are reversed, with parrot teaching parront about what matters most in life, where to look for it, and how to cling to it when you find it—with wings, beak, and all eight (five if you are Pearl) sharp claws.

<u>Lessons with Wings</u>: *I "practice" meditation. Pearl lives it. He takes none of life for granted. Whatever is in front of him in each moment must be the thing he is meant to focus on. If someone looks at him and says "pretty birdie" he chirps—maybe he knows what they are saying and maybe he doesn't, but he thoroughly enjoys the attention just the same. Ironically, I miss Pearl terribly during the month I live in Cape Cod each year. But he is as happy as a, well, parrot, chirping away with all the birds at Ray's Birdie Hotel, where he shares a home with parrotlets, a mustache parakeet, several finches, and countless professional singing canaries.*

What's Yours is Mine

Pearl, like every feathered companion I have kept company with to date, has a very egalitarian view of the world.

I call this avian credo "What's Yours is Mine."

Loosely translated (just in case you're actually confused) this credo means that what's his is his...with an addendum that what's mine is also his. With pure application, the credo extends to family, friends, and strangers as well. If Pearl wants it, it must be his. During the years I was still living at home with my folks, more than one surprised dinner guest learned the hard way that disagreeing with a determined avian might not result in the loss of your dinner plate, but it most certainly can result in the loss of your desire for it.

The credo also applies to electronics, apparel, reading material, household decorations, and more. Pearl's sole responsibility here in invoking "What's Yours is Mine" is to comb through everything in "my" possession, whether it be the snacks on my plate, the garments in my closet, the supplies in my office drawer, the contents of my purse, or the magazines stacked in my magazine rack. Once he has conducted a thorough inventory, he is then well informed enough to select the things he wants. He indicates an item has been selected by pooping on it, chewing holes in it, sitting on it for long periods of time (his fuzzy light blue bathrobe hanging in our closet is a great example of this), consuming it, or all of the above.

The credo gets more interesting—and complicated—when it comes to carving out personal territory on the home turf.

Over the years Pearl and I have moved on several occasions, during which time we have worked out a system of sorts for selecting which areas of a new space are specifically "ours." First, I pick out a temporary place to install Pearl. Next, he systematically checks out the rest of the new casa, evaluating each potential perch, niche, or nook in turn. He lets me know which area he wants to check out next in repetitive and extremely unsubtle ways—with shrieking, head gestures, and a curious kind of clinging thing he does where he grips my shirt with his few small claws and hangs off the edge of the fabric, wings flapping uselessly but vigorously in the direction he wants to go.

As a last resort he will take off in the general direction of his intended destination, enduring a predictably vertical trajectory as gravity takes its course. He will then land awkwardly and either start to walk towards the selected spot or shriek for me to come and pick him up and take him there (at least by then I am usually pretty well informed about where he wants to go). Frequently his chosen location features that rarest and most precious of commodities—a reflective surface. It often also has other desirable amenities—for instance, a tasty forbidden green houseplant to nibble on, a comfy wide round towel rack to perch on, or a crunchy wicker basket to dismantle.

Sometimes Pearl selects an item I have also selected. This can be challenging. Under the longstanding complementary "Avian Right of First Refusal" rule, the item is automatically Pearl's until he decides otherwise. So the best I can usually hope for is to work out some kind of time-sharing arrangement. For instance, I can wear the fuzzy light blue bathrobe my mom bought me for Christmas when Pearl is: a) sitting on something else I used to own that is equally soft and comfy, b) tunneling through the center of what was originally going to be my waffle breakfast, c) admiring his reflection in my (our) laptop screen, or d) napping in the sun on his "cockatiel run" (aka the window ledge). Sometimes we can both use the item at the same time, such as when I am wearing his light blue bathrobe but he is also sitting on my shoulder while I wear it. These types of mutual win-win negotiations are great resume builders, as they call for the sorts of creative problem-solving approaches that can make time-suck meetings feel productive and convince bosses you are actually doing company work at your desk rather than writing a blog about your pet bird on the internet.

While it might seem like a sacrifice to grow up, work hard, and finally be able to buy all the stuff you coveted when you were little and broke, only to then be forced by a featherweight housemate to assume the beta role in your own household, I can say from personal experience that "beta" is a far more satisfying position than its reputation might suggest. I love it when I tell a cute story about my bird and a listener snarks, "He sure is spoiled!" I always want to ask these folks what they think the primary reason is for bringing home an animal companion.

But I doubt I'd stick around long enough to hear their answer.

<u>Lessons with Wings</u>: *It feels good to let the rules go, indulge a loved one, laugh at harmless no-no's as they are being carried out. When I was a child I delighted in the lure of the forbidden, but as an adult I somehow justify expecting myself to constantly stay within the lines, to be responsible, to "be productive," even if I am the only one who notices or cares. Thank goodness I had the wisdom to bring Pearl into my life! With his help, I can learn—on a daily basis—which rules are actually worth keeping and which rules are simply made for the joy of breaking them.*

Waffles for One

I have a confession to make. My bird likes scrambled eggs.

At first, I didn't pay much attention to this preference. In fact, I'm pretty sure I gave it no thought at all until a Facebook friend delicately pointed out that, um, Pearl came from an, um, egg... Until my friend mentioned this, I just thought watching Pearl bury his beak into a delicious pile of scrambled eggs was cute. Now I think it is cute and creepy.

For the record, "scrambled eggs" is not the only breakfast dish Pearl enjoys. He readily ingests a wide range of other breakfasty-type delicacies as well, including crepes, watermelon, toast, biscuits, and most especially waffles. This last preference has made him somewhat of a social media celebrity. Apparently "waffle" is not a common victuals choice for domesticated avians.

In the course of his growing celebrity status, I have often been questioned by his fans about whether Pearl prefers his waffles plain, with butter, with fruit, or with maple syrup. Shudder. PLAIN. Definitely plain. Just the thought of maple syrup + feathers makes me feel queasy. I have also fielded a number of questions on Pearl's behalf about which brand of waffles he enjoys most. This is an easy question to answer: Mom's. He will tunnel right through the center of one of my mom's homemade organic waffles, but turn up his beak at the sight of my expensive Whole Foods organic waffles. (Don't even ask about Eggo® et al. Store bought assembly line waffles get a consistently wide berth from us both.)

While Pearl vastly prefers fresh-off-the-griddle, piping hot Mom's waffles, he will accept re-heated Mom's waffles if absolutely necessary. When we are at his grandparents' house, usually all he has to do to receive a waffle for his very own is slide down my dad's shirtsleeve and jump into the middle of his plate (not surprisingly, at this point Dad never displays even a hint of reluctance to hand over the chosen waffle). When we are at home, however, he employs his own trademarked three-step process to attack and dismantle a waffle.

First, he plants his feet (if you can imagine a teensy sumo wrestler in his itsy-bitsy wrestling bikini positioning his feet firmly on the mat, you will get a good visual of the proper avian waffle-eating stance). Next, he selects a spot inside the perimeter of the waffle, usually slightly off-center, from which to anchor his efforts. From there, he proceeds to use his beak like a tiny spade to tunnel right through the center of the waffle, alternately consuming and flinging waffle particles as he goes.

Once he is full, the sole remaining step is to perform the classic "head shake with beak fling." Like a hearty burp after a fine French meal, this necessary housekeeping task removes any stray unsightly waffle fragments that may still be clinging to the top of his beak while also giving the chef an accurate assessment of how much he enjoyed his meal. Waffle fragments on the tabletop indicate mild enjoyment. Waffle fragments on the neighbor's front porch indicate a five-star gourmet experience.

Perhaps most endearing of all is this—each day is a new, great day for waffles in Pearl's world. Turns out that breakfast really is the most important meal of the day.

<u>Lessons with Wings</u>: *Life offers many simple joys. For Pearl, waffles qualify. For me, watching Pearl eat waffles qualifies. But unlike his mommy, Pearl never takes life's daily joys for granted. Each day presents a fresh round of lovely gifts to enjoy, and each day he is equally excited about these gifts...a perspective I am determined to learn to emulate.*

Why I Don't Volunteer for the SPCA

A few years ago, I did a short stint as a volunteer with the Wildlife Center of Texas.

The Wildlife Center, while affiliated with the Society for the Prevention of Cruelty to Animals (SPCA) of Texas, cares only for wildlife and not for domesticated animals.

While volunteering for the Wildlife Center, my official job description was "baby bird feeder." Unlike adult bird feeders, which you can just hang on tree limbs and refill after the squirrels have eaten all the birdseed yet again, motherless baby birds need their human stand-ins to do things like dangling legless plump grasshopper bodies in front of their tiny beaks until instincts kick in and ingestion occurs.

I learned a lot during my time at the Wildlife Center, including that scientists are right about corvids (jays, crows, ravens, and the like) being amongst the smartest of all non-human species (avian or non-avian). If ever a volunteer was witnessed hightailing it around the room after an escaped baby bird, it was usually a corvid baby they were trying to catch. Every corvid I ever fed kept one eye on the grasshopper and one eye on the door. "Opportunity can knock twice" is the corvid's official motto. Why settle for just lunch when you can get lunch and your freedom, too?

While I thoroughly enjoyed my season of feeding the wild birds at the Wildlife Center, I know better than to volunteer to care for their domestic counterparts at our local SPCA. Reason being? I am a pushover. I know I am not the only parront with this problem either. In fact, the last book I read about a pet bird started with the author owning one parrot. By the end of the book, the author (who volunteers regularly with her local SPCA) owned four parrots. This is approximately three parrots more than Pearl will permit. We have a code. Actually it is not a written code per se but more like a guideline. "Thou shalt cohabitate with only one parrot" pretty much sums up the guideline. To date, I have not observed the guideline to be flexible.

Recently I went out of town for five weeks for our annual family vacation to Cape Cod. During this time I decided to ignore my "no SPCA" rule—temporarily. I made this decision in the interests of personal health and wellbeing, since by that time Pearl and I had been separated for quite some weeks and I was starting to experience avian-related delirium tremens. However, the moment I walked in the doors of the Massachusetts SPCA and heard the familiar screeching sounds I knew I had made a mistake. There he was— "Salty," a four-year-old yellow cockatiel, recently returned after not one but two unsuccessful prior adoption experiences. My heart melted. The SPCA staff told me his story, which didn't help any. Apparently, despite what they told the SPCA, the people who had adopted Salty previously did not understand how to handle pet parrots. Consequently, Salty came back to the SPCA with an ever-deepening fear of perches, fingers, and other long thin objects. He also became "cage territorial," a term which means he has trouble entering and exiting his cage and he acts very possessive whenever he is in, on, or near his cage.

So basically, Salty has problems.

And now I had problems, because I instinctively understood these learned fears were a great source of distress to this sweet and loving bird. Salty is a hand-fed cockatiel who was born and bred for domesticated life as a companion bird to humans. Even in the short time we spent together, I quickly realized Salty understood the simple commands all hand-fed cockatiel babies are taught— commands like "step up"—very well. So he was eager to comply but scared of what he had to step up onto, which in nearly every case consisted of a perch, a finger, or (best case scenario) an arm. He was simultaneously so eager and so scared that I often witnessed how, upon hearing the command "step up," he would leap *over* my arm in his efforts to find a workable compromise. Once successfully perched on my shoulder, Salty would dip his head to ask me to scratch his itchy neck feathers, but then when he would see my long, thin, perch-like fingers coming up to comply with his request he would get scared and bite me.

Like Pearl, Salty is a "special needs" cockatiel and I quickly became convinced I was Salty's own miracle worker.

But it could not be. There is the code, and its "one parrot per household" rule. The moral of this story is, don't volunteer with the SPCA unless you are absolutely prepared to own several parrots. At least if you are me.

<u>Lessons with Wings</u>: *At this precise moment as I type, I have just sent an email to a newly established domestic avian rescue organization near my house. In my email, I inquired if I might be of service as a volunteer. I hope they say yes. It was very difficult to leave Salty to return home to Houston, but the SPCA staff assured me I had made a positive difference in his life—even if I couldn't adopt him myself. Not every parrot is so fortunate to have a loving home like my Pearl. I can't adopt every parrot I meet, but this doesn't mean I can't help make their lives better by volunteering to clean cages, change food and water, and play with parrots who are waiting to be adopted.*

Show Bird

From time to time, groups of parrot-loving featherless beings enjoy getting together en masse with their avians. When this occurs, the featherless beings are free range and the avians are behind bars.

The primary purpose of these gatherings is to decide which avians are the prettiest. Like most appearance-based contests, judging prettiness revolves around a type of point system. Points are awarded for different categories of prettiness—crests, wings, tail, coloration, and (a real point-killer if you happen to be Pearl) posture and deportment.

As I have told my friends at the National Cockatiel Society, I could never judge these contests. If I served as a judge all of the contestants would win First Place. If a Grand Prize was awarded for prettiness, they would all win that, too. This is because, to me, all parrots are very pretty. Just having parrot DNA makes you automatically pretty in my opinion.

But even if we had any delusions of ribbon-related grandeur, Pearl's three missing claws and permanently damaged left wing currently makes that goal unrealistic at best. Reason being—modern show bird standards classify these as "faults" (sort of like my curvy Polish-Armenian figure and 5'6" stature are currently considered faults should I ever aspire to launch a modeling career).

Luckily, just like a frown is a smile turned upside down, to us a left wing that prevents flight just means Mom carries you everywhere—both saving you energy and keeping you well accustomed to the life of luxury you so richly deserve. In the same way, possessing an hourglass figure simply means you never have to wonder where the "belt" should go in that day's chosen ensemble.

When we do feel the need for a bit of competitive excitement, we can stand together in front of a mirror and compete with each other for the title of "Prettiest."

Here, of course, Pearl wins every time, since we are both judges and we both unanimously agree he is the prettiest.

<u>Lessons with Wings</u>: *"Prettiness," too, is a relative term. For instance (believe it or not) some people can actually look at an avian—parrot or otherwise—and fail to see total prettiness. In the same way, some people have not yet developed the eyes to see prettiness in themselves and/or others. I myself didn't have this gift for many years. Luckily, today I share my life with a being who sees prettiness wherever he looks, and he is teaching me to do the same.*

Peace

I have a friend who told me that when she got her two kittens she was able to stop taking her anxiety meds.

Even though you couldn't pry my anxiety meds out of my cold dead hands (my family and friends all agree we like my new personality) I can see her point. There is little in life more peace-inducing than kissing your parrot's soft feathery head or delivering yet another (repeat, highly anticipated) neck feather massage.

It is a fact that I often try to arrange my daily life so as to have as much peace as possible. I try to keep my relationships simple and my home life simpler. If I am thinking of moving to a new place, I may (do) obsessively drive by it several (hundreds of) times—even after I've signed the lease—just to reassure myself once and for all that it is "quiet enough." Yet inside my head, more frequently the exact opposite reigns supreme. Apparently I am not a peaceful being by nature. I am a reasonably intelligent being, a motivated being, a caring being, a creative being, a well-intentioned being—but a naturally peaceful being I most definitely am not.

I wouldn't say Pearl is particularly peaceful either. Parrots in general seem to favor the "high alert" setting over more balanced responses to life—or perhaps they don't have much biological choice in the matter. What I mean by this is: my bird can see a winged predator wheeling so high above us that even with my prescription glasses I can barely make out a tiny dark airborne dot. As well, he seems effortlessly attuned to the subtlest shifts in sound, air pressure, daylight, shapes (in particular, Pearl shows a strong preference for the "cockatiel" shape and an equally strong aversion to the "hawk" shape) as well as the comings and goings of the other beings all around him. I don't know that he especially wants to be aware of any or all of these things—yet he is innately aware just the same.

This is probably why "Peace" is one of the six words that made it all the way through the "annual word run-offs" and into its own tiny silver paper clip on this year's word wall. Neither Pearl nor I may be especially peaceful in our essential character. Nevertheless, we both remain quite dedicated to the challenge of enticing peace into our lair and convincing it to stay.

Don't Worry

Some people like to hang inspirational slogans ("Dance Like Nobody's Watching," "With God All Things Are Possible," et al) in their kitchen or over their front door.

If Pearl and I decided to decorate in this fashion, there is no doubt in my mind what our chosen slogan would be: "Don't Worry." We would likely need to post it in every room, too…and probably more than once per room just to be safe.

Interestingly, I have noticed that birds in general, most being mouthful-sized and fairly delicious to a large number of natural predators, tend to come with a nervous nature pre-installed. Whether foraging for food, choosing a mate, constructing a nest, tending young, snoozing, or simply gliding on the wind, "high alert" seems to be the preferred setting for staying both aloft and alive.

My domesticated sidekick is no exception. While he certainly doesn't have to contend with the perils of the great outdoors like his wild counterparts do, this hasn't affected the factory preset one bit. To the contrary, he starts instinctively worrying the moment I move out of sight—will Mom ever come back? If I don't move fast enough to lift him to view a preferred reflective surface—will he ever get to see it? When a head-butt doesn't deliver the requested neck feather scratches right away—will his neck feathers always be itchy? When he wants my grilled cheese sandwich and I appear to also want it—will it ever be his?

In a human child or my parents' lethargic standard dachshund, J.P. Morgan, a sudden overactive anxiety reflex might present as just cause for corrective therapy. In Pearl, however, I am simply witnessing the evolutionary building blocks of natural selection at its finest. Avians who devote sufficient energy to productive worry are likely to live longer than their flock mates and produce more anxious little avians to make Darwin proud.

As well (providing yet more circumstantial evidence that pets and owners choose one another for complementary personalities as much as for similar looks) my own worry setting could give Pearl's a run for its money any day of the week. I justify this by claiming the things I worry about—earning cash, that angry-looking red blotch on my thigh, loneliness in my old age—are higher-level worries than Pearl's. But in truth it is all relative to our respective cases. Pearl will continue to worry about what Pearl worries about—itchy neck feathers, the dwindling worldwide waffle supply, that nasty man in the white lab coat with the surgical gloves and feather clippers.

I, too, will continue to worry about what I worry about. With "Don't Worry" as our motto and our battle cry, back to back we will continue to creep forward into the fray of life, eyes down, shoulders hunched, beaks, claws, and pepper spray at the ready, taking one preventative, anxious step at a time.

<u>Lessons with Wings</u>: *For years I blamed, shamed, and judged myself for my so-called "overly anxious" nature. Even worse, I often allowed others to do the same. But then I met Pearl, my anxiety soulmate. Pearl (unlike me) is not ashamed of being high strung. In his life, worry frequently serves a useful and even life-sustaining function. As well (and again unlike his mommy) when his anxiety has served its purpose, he discards it instantly and goes right back to enjoying whatever he was doing before the hawk flew by/waffle was withdrawn/Mom temporarily moved out of direct line-of-sight. This has been one of my most helpful lessons to date about managing anxiety. Thanks to Pearl's example, I am starting to see that anxiety is just a messenger. Sometimes the message is relevant and worthy of my instant and undivided attention. Sometimes the message isn't worth a second thought. Either way, my sole role is to receive the message, open it, review it, decide what to do, and then let the message (and its messenger) go.*

(Im)patience is a Virtue

"Later" is not a concept parrots understand. "Now" is the only time.

This means delay tactics are fruitless in a parront's world. There is no bargaining, no wiggle room on the timing of what happens when in the daily schedule. There is no daily schedule. There is also no "punishment" or "reward"—as in, "I'm so sorry you didn't enjoy your vet visit but here is some crunchy millet to make up for it." The vet visit still sucked and the millet is still tasty. What does one have to do with the other?

Similarly, what is the point in delaying the start of fun activities like shredding Mommy's wicker couch frame, admiring your reflection in the refrigerator handles, dismantling a fresh and delicious toasted waffle, shrieking at the wild birds outside, enjoying the view from one of several panoramic window ledges or exploring the interior of a bag full of crunchy chips? If an interesting opportunity presents itself, it must be on the agenda for right now.

If you have a pet you probably already appreciate the peculiar charm and vulnerability of what Eckhart Tolle likes to call "The Power of Now" and Pearl prefers to simply act out. For instance, if we ran and stuck our whole face in our dinner bowl the moment the meal was served, our dinner mates would probably at the very least politely turn (or run) away. But when excitement outpaces etiquette in my avian sidekick yet again, I oooh and ahhh like any proud parront would. Sometimes I even snap pictures and post them on Facebook so other parronts can oooh and ahhh with me.

But perhaps more significantly, I also learn a valuable lesson each time this happens. Even ignoring the obvious (i.e., my lengthy prior years' battle with an eating disorder, depression, and anxiety), again and again I discover how something compelling and delightful occurs whenever pure innocence encounters pure enthusiasm. Perhaps this is why we as a species are so keen to procreate the moment our reproductive powers get activated. Without offspring around to remind us, it becomes all too easy to lose our childlike appreciation of the simplest joys in life as we juggle lightweight co-workers, a mate with a housework allergy, and a mortgage.

And while it is always possible to pick up a book and read what somebody else has learned about "now" or "impatience" or whatever we prefer to call it, it is much easier as well as more fun to absorb the lesson when it is staged with sound effects and a live action cast right in front of us...especially if one of the (very cute and talented) actors just happens to have feathers.

Thanks to Pearl, I have slowly begun to appreciate the allure of the joie de vivre tucked inside small acts of healthy impatience. While it doesn't work in all situations, and certainly there is a reason why one of us is continually assigned to play the matron's role while the other one of us gets to reprise the ingénue yet again, in the grand scheme of things, "why wait" certainly has its place.

In other words, that fresh-baked hand-cut donut won't always be there, and neither will the chance to start the first eating disorders mentoring organization, celebrate a dear friend's birthday, move to India...or simply spend the balance of a relaxing afternoon scratching soft neck feathers.

<u>Lessons with Wings</u>: *Most of life can wait. Truly. It can. I am already quite sure that when I am lying on my deathbed I will not regret not spending more time cleaning the casa or sitting at my desk working. What I WILL regret is putting off until later simple pleasures I can enjoy (and share) today.*

1001 Ways a Cockatiel Can Die

This is not a pleasant subject.

Which—of course—is exactly why I bring it up.

Just as I share my love of my parrot with my fellow parronts, so too am I realizing we share many of the same fears. Sometimes talking about our fears neutralizes them. Sometimes it at least puts them in their proper place. Sometimes it does none of these things—but I figure it's worth a shot.

In fact, just the other day (after yet another particularly terrifying dream about bad things happening to my very good parrot) I confided in a friend that I was afraid I might love Pearl too much. He responded, "Yes, you kiss him too much." This, obviously, was not at all what I was getting at.

Rather, while I do not have human kids I mother and worry about, I mother and worry about my avian "fid" (feathery + kid) just as much. I worry he will have a night fright, bang his fragile left wing, and bleed out. I worry he will fly down to the floor (where his flying, er, skills inevitably take him) and encounter pest poisons, angry spiders, non-feathery pets, or a human foot before I can scoop him to safety. I worry he will eat something toxic (paint, grout, metal—all of which parrots think are tasty and parronts know are poisonous) and expire, with the vet and his mommy standing by helpless to save him.

I worry someone will break into my house and hurt him (note that here I spend much more time worrying the criminal will hurt him than I do worrying the criminal will hurt me). I worry he will turn his head the wrong way while I'm scratching his neck feathers and I will do him an injury, or worse. I worry he will be stolen or set "free" (aka released into a place where three squares, spring water refills, and fresh new cage paper do not arrive at preset hours throughout the day). I worry his "leak-proof" water bottle will spring a sudden leak and he will irreversibly dehydrate before I get home to refill it.

And I worry about oh-so-many other things...sooooo many other things. Sometimes I joke to friends and fellow parronts (although seldom to Pearl's grandparents, who make me look like amateur hour in the worry department) that I have a running dream series called "1001 Ways a Cockatiel Can Die." They think it is funny.

I think it is true.

<u>Lessons with Wings</u>: *There is just so much time and energy I can spend worrying about Pearl before a) it takes away from my ability to enjoy life with Pearl, and b) that worry becomes selfish and self-serving. When I feel myself crossing the line from genuine concern about Pearl's quality of life into the territory of "what will I do/how will I cope without Pearl in my life?" I know it is time to rein my worrying in. Worry can be a survival tool—it can help me to identify potential dangers/toxins/situations my parrot (and his mommy) should avoid. But when worry becomes unproductive (aka paranoid) it has outlived its instinctual survival purpose and taken on an unhealthy life of its own. This is when I know I must moderate my fears about Pearl's safety if I want to be able to fully enjoy the precious gift of our daily life together.*

Finches...and Why We Don't Have Any

It has always been my goal to work from home.

For starters, mornings suck (or at least they do if you have my DNA). Also, jammies are very comfortable. Perhaps most importantly, I like selecting my own office mates, and I much prefer it if they have feathers. But several years ago I went through a period where, try as I might, each job I got seemed to come with a mandatory away-from-home office attached. I was out of the house a LOT. And a certain feathery someone didn't like it one bit.

I was getting worried Pearl was too lonely during the day, so the next time I dropped him off at the birdie hotel before a business trip, I asked my breeder friend Ray for advice. Ray suggested getting a pair of Zebra finches (what he actually said was, "They're only $5 and I can get two for you at the bird show next month.") He made it sound so easy. Then I went online and researched "Zebra finches" and discovered they cohabitate with cockatiels in the wild.

This was starting to sound like the perfect solution.

A few weeks later, Ray called and told me the finches—both male birds—had at last arrived. I drove over to get them—two tiny cute brown and white striped powder puffs with even tinier orange beaks and itty-bitty long orange legs. After watching them for a few minutes as they zipped around their shiny white cage while calling to each other nonstop, I named them "Tweety" and "Taz." When we got back home I placed their cage next to Pearl's and waited for the bonding to begin.

While I waited, Pearl and I got a crash course in Zebra finch behavior. For instance, Zebra finches can projectile poop in any direction—even while flying (and even while flying upside down).

Zebra finches make parrots look like neat, patient, refined diners. Zebra finches are tone-deaf, and their, er, song never varies by more than an excruciating half tone up or down—ever. Zebra finches also never stop "singing." Zebra finches respond to conference calls, daytime naps, migraine headaches, and television programs with an automatic volume increase. Zebra finches can (and do) eat (and fling) their body weight in finch food—hourly. Zebra finches react to all attempts to feed, clean, or care for them as if their safety, the safety of their children, and the safety of their children's children is being threatened. Zebra finches will try to make an egg—in public and all day long—whether or not the requisite male-female finch pairing is present. A single "healthy finch" vet checkup costs more than an entire aviary's worth of actual Zebra finches.

Perhaps most pertinently, while my internet research did absolutely confirm cockatiels and Zebra finches share a habitat in the wild, nothing I read said anything about them liking one another. To Tweety and Taz, Pearl seemed about as harmless as an incoming nuclear missile. As well, outside of occasionally using this to his advantage, Pearl most often appeared to be attempting to forcibly will both finches out of existence.

One day I took all three birds over to my folks' house for a thorough double cage cleaning. While I was otherwise occupied cleaning around the door of the finch casa, Tweety saw his chance and made a break for it—making it all the way outdoors and up into the tall trees ringing my folks' back fence before I even registered what that tiny brown blur streaking past me had been. Taz was heartbroken. We tried for hours to use the caged Taz as "bait" to lure Tweety back inside…to no avail. Finally it got dark and we had to give up. Tweety remained in the treetops for the next couple of days as my mom made periodic attempts to recapture him. But he always eluded her. Finally, he disappeared for good.

When I told Ray, he suggested we simply replace Tweety with another Zebra finch. While Ray hunted around for Tweety #2, I indulged in escalating fantasies about returning to my now blissfully remembered pre-finch days. Finally, I guiltily shared my anti-finch sentiments with Mom and Dad, who not so guiltily shared them with

Ray, who sweetly offered to assist with finch fostering services until a suitable new home could be found. By the time Tweety #2 arrived, both finches were on target for placement in the home of some actual finch lovers.

I celebrated in suitable style of course. First I cleaned the bathroom from top to bottom. Next I cleaned the whole house from top to bottom.

Then I laid down for a restful mid-day nap, lured by the magically silent strains of a permanently finch-free future.

<u>Lessons with Wings</u>: *Taking in a new pet is a serious commitment. I had assumed—wrongly—that because a) I love birds, b) I love Pearl, c) I had loved all my previous parrots, d) I would also love living with finches. How wrong I was. As well, I took them in purely for Pearl's sake and not for their own or mine. When little Taz got his foot tangled up in finch nesting material and I actually found myself asking the vet for a price quote before bringing him in, I realized my mistake and took immediate steps to repair it by finding the finches a new and more suitable home. I am so glad I realized I am a "one bird mommy"—for all our sakes and for the sake of any future companion birds I may contemplate inviting to share Pearl's life...and my own.*

Shriek Fest

Several years ago I was on an airplane traveling home after a speaking event.

As I took my seat, I noticed that a few rows behind me sat a mom with her young child. A distinguished-looking businessman soon arrived to occupy the seat to my right. To my left, an athletically built young man in possession of an enviably large set of noise-cancelling headphones was already emitting soft snores.

And I was in hell. For starters, there was the whole issue of middle seats and whether maintaining an affinity for personal space marked me as hopelessly old-fashioned. Add to this the continually changing in-flight air pressure wreaking havoc with a certain set of young eardrums, causing ever-escalating rounds of shrieking. Finally I had had it. I turned around. Glared. Uttered audible and very targeted unkind words towards the eardrums in question.

At which point the businessman beside me calmly stated, "You must not have children." "No I don't," I replied (wondering how he had guessed). "I have three at home. I don't even hear the shrieking anymore," he told me. This was a revelation. My first thought was to beg the nice gentleman to make an appointment with his audiologist because clearly there was something wrong with his ears.

But today, I have a different take on his words. This is because, today, I have 12 years' worth of parronting under my belt. Speaking of parenting, when I was little, my folks made up wonderful nicknames for me like "Shannabanana." It seems worth noting these are the exact same people who have since nicknamed their beloved grandbird "The Little Shrieker."

We Cuttses call it like we see it.

Truthfully (and just as that businessman described) today I no longer even hear the shrieking. There are two reasons for this. Reason number one: the shrieking no longer sounds like shrieking to me. Rather, when Pearl calls, what I hear is my companion expressing his needs, "warning" his "flock" about imminent dangers, expressing a desire for my company, telling me he's tired and many more important messages as well. Reason number two: when I signed up to become a parront, I also willingly signed up for all the responsibilities my role requires—including a healthy daily dose of shriek-based communications.

Plus I can't help but admit it is not a one-way street. Sometimes I yell at my refrigerator (occasionally I also kick). Pearl has to listen to this—at times he even joins in for a supportive round or two. If he can tolerate my version of shrieking, the least I can do is extend the same courtesy in return. In fact, I can only imagine how odd my full range of oh-so-human noises sounds to his birdie ears—the humming, the off-key singing, the thinly disguised cursing, the sobbing, the grumbling…but not once has he ever complained.

The truth is, I will never, ever, grow tired of the sound of Pearl's voice—whether he is using it to express love, fear, anger, frustration, or a simple shrieking version of "Welcome home, Mom!"

Lessons with Wings: *We all shriek—each in our own way. Similarly, we are all called upon to tolerate the shrieks of others…albeit with varying degrees of success and empathy on any given day. As a single adult, I could have chosen not to have a pet. But in that choice I would have cheated myself of the chance to learn some of life's most valuable lessons—lessons about commitment, interdependence, tolerance, unconditional love, communication, and so many more. Plus, in choosing life with Pearl, I get daily, full-immersion interspecies language lessons totally free of charge. Bonus!*

Fling It

If non-humans were allowed to compete in the Olympic games, parrots would be a natural for events like the discus throw, which basically entails flinging random objects far distances for fun and profit.

Not only would allowing parrot entrants add newfound spice and variety to the competition, but it would also serve to keep prize money costs low. I say this because (at least if my own bird is any indication) parrots appear to enjoy this activity so much they are willing to do it for free.

In anticipation of the first interspecies Olympics, Pearl has been practicing his discus moves daily by flinging birdseed, waffle crumbs, and, of course, anything he wants to see me bend down and pick up. Like babies, parrots are always up for a rousing round of "I drop it and you pick it up," complete with escalating challenge levels. This serves to lend variety to training sessions while ensuring the trainer never forgets how much she hates squats.

Of course, to become an Olympic-worthy discus thrower it is necessary to train regularly. Since a parrot's motto is "anything worth doing is worth doing over and over again," this can quickly translate into lots of training time. It can also be helpful to train with many different flingable items to refine your technique. For example, let's say someone in the household is about to dig into a tasty plate of al dente-style spaghetti noodles—noodles which appear to be perfect for discus training. So first, the athlete must select the noodles with the best shape and size for his training session.

As soon as a suitable noodle selection has been made, it is then time for a preparatory activity known as "consumption." The athlete's goal during the consumption stage is twofold: a) to build up physical strength by filling the belly with noodles, and b) to ensure there is sufficient noodle consumption to provide for an evenly dense noodle particle build-up all along the outer edges of the beak.

When the beak build-up has reached the appropriate height, width, and density, it is then time to initiate the final "head shake." Here, the best discus athletes' head shakes incorporate both shaking and twisting of the head and neck and full body movement (a similar analogy might be when a golfer is instructed to use the entire body to swing the golf club). A properly performed Olympic-grade head shake will distribute noodle particles fairly evenly across all surfaces up and out to a certain distance. Taking daily measurements of noodle particle distribution, density, and distance can then be used as helpful benchmarks for progress in training.

Pearl's last training session left noodle fragments sticking to the carpet, drying on the glass tabletop, congealed on nearby windows, and clinging to my hair. Clearly, he is making great progress. Now all that remains is to wait for the Olympic Committee to see the light and adjust its criteria to include worthy interspecies contenders.

For now, my Olympic hopeful is once again engaged in his favorite post-training session activity—polishing his medal-worthy beak on his proud mommy's t-shirt.

Lessons with Wings: *It is great to set and achieve goals in life. But it is equally great to simply enjoy the process of setting and working towards those goals. When I was still struggling to recover from my eating disorder, I was soooo impatient to "get well already." I just wanted it over and done with. At that time in my life, I didn't want to "enjoy the journey," "trust the process," or accept "progress not perfection." Blech. But Pearl doesn't have a problem with any of these things. This is because, for Pearl, life isn't about setting or even achieving goals. For Pearl, life is about LIVING. It is about waking up for another day just because you can and because you never know what fun new adventures might await. And with Pearl, there are always fun new adventures that await!*

House Rules

No long jumping into the middle of other diners' plates.
No feeding the mirrors your breakfast.
No admiring yourself in the shiny rims of the stove burners.
No unauthorized flights.
No chewing on power cables.
No cleaning your beak on Mommy's laptop.

These are just a few of the house rules that, in theory, can turn any household containing at least one avian and at least one human into a restful, safe, and anxiety-free home. In fact, thus far there has been no actual proof this theory is true.

Yet the list continues to grow longer. Perhaps this is because, as I continue to make up new house rules and Pearl continues to break them, we are both growing older, and my parront's eyes are growing ever keener in spotting potential dangers I think my parrot should avoid. However, parrots (unlike humans) do not seem to notice the passage of time or their own advancing age. This gift appears to keep them both young at heart and richly supplied with inspiration and moxie. It would seem only logical then that life with Pearl has the potential to do the same for me...if I could manage to cease and desist from worrying my life away cataloguing all the things that could prematurely interrupt his.

Most of the time as I worry, Pearl is happily exploring the heights of yet another windowsill ledge, chirping appreciatively to his reflection in the narrow shower door rim, rearranging strands of gently-used dental floss into his own customized designs, and all manner of other perilously off-limits activities. He sees opportunity and adventure. I see certain doom. Yet one of us has a lifespan of approximately 20 years and the other one (at least if family history holds true) has a lifespan of approximately 100 years. If self-confidence, a positive outlook, and an adventurous spirit could predict longevity, it is not difficult to guess who would then outlive whom.

For instance, as I type I am worrying that you, the reader, may fail to sufficiently grasp the singular charm of my avian's character due to the deficiencies of his biographer. Pearl, on the other hand, is making great progress with this morning's project of tunneling to the next galaxy through the interior of his wicker basket. Lined with crunchy editorials I have already read (I wasn't born yesterday), and decorated with tiny celebratory bright mirrors, tinkling bells, sparkly Mardi Gras beads, and other enticing artifacts, at this precise moment his tail is pointing skyward as he repositions himself to get a more favorable grip on a choice interior section of tasty wicker. Beak wrestling sharp individual pieces of wicker wood is a firm "no-no" on the house rules list. Yet Pearl has assembled a tidy little pile of these exact pointy pieces in the front right corner of his basket—the corner located closest to his mommy's keenly watchful eyes.

The other day I read on Wikipedia that cockatiels can live as long as 36 years. Or at least one cockatiel in one documented study reportedly lived that long. The very next sentence then talked about the importance of diet and exercise relative to lifespan. Speaking of which (and despite his mommy's best efforts otherwise), once again this morning Pearl breakfasted on birdseed....and birdseed. His exercise today thus far has consisted of shrieking, preening-in-place, and napping on the windowsill. Yet here we are—he is 12 and I am 42, and both of us are actually holding up rather well given how precisely (or not) we are following our respective recommended daily guidelines for just about everything.

So for now, I will continue worrying and he will continue giving me something to worry about. And perhaps, in time, time itself will reveal that the secret to living a record number of years isn't so much what you do or don't do, but with whom you are doing it.

In which case we can both look forward to a long and happy life…together.

Lessons with Wings: *Within MentorCONNECT, the nonprofit community I founded, we often say, "relationships replace eating disorders." This basically means that the more supportive connections a recovering person has, the better their odds of recovery are likely to be. In the same way, close and loving relationships of any kind can reconfigure all sorts of daunting odds in favor of those who are doing the loving and relating. Pearl and I are clearly living proof of this.*

Love...With a Side of Feathers

Signing up for life with a parrot basically means signing up for a life with feathers.

Sometimes this is oh-so-precious. Say your feathery sidekick is sitting on his favorite ledge preening. Suddenly, a downy breast feather exits his midsection and floats down to the floor. You bend over and pick it up, marveling all the while at such ethereal softness.

At other times this may seem slightly less precious. Let's say your feathery sidekick is sitting on your shoulder preening. Suddenly the microwave dings and your freshly brewed jasmine tea is ready. You take a deep, delicious sip, only to find yourself mindlessly gumming... something. Upon further inspection, the mystery garnish reveals itself to be a mangled wet downy breast feather.

Luckily, after you get back home from the coffee shop with your overpriced breast feather-free coffee, you still have enough time to complete your morning routine of sweeping up crest, chest, wing, and tail feathers...along with a generous helping of powdery white feather dust and—of course—parrot poop.

Then, approximately one hour later (give or take an hour), it is time for round two—because the moment you pick up the broom to sweep up what has just been preened out, your parrot takes this as the universally-recognized signal to begin the process of crest-to-tail full body grooming all over again. In between preening sessions your parrot will probably want you to scratch his neck feathers to remove the waxy keratin sheaths from new emerging pinfeathers. When you are finished with this task, your parrot will enjoy displaying his shiny new feathers while you enjoy the vigorous physical exercise of cleaning waxy keratin particles off of, well, everything.

Molting season makes regular parrot preening procedures look like a warm-up act. Scientists tell us that every seven years each cell in our body is replaced with a brand new one. Replace cells with feathers and humans with parrots, substitute every few months for every seven years, and you now have a pretty good "big picture" overview of the molting process. In the wild, the purpose of the full body molt is to ensure all feathers are fresh and new for routine and extended migratory flight. In captivity, the purpose of the full body molt is to ensure the entire household receives at least three to four ceiling-to-floor cleanings annually.

Speaking of which, if you enjoy those guessing games like the ones where there are X number of marbles in a jar, you will love the game "Guess the Number of Feathers on the Bird." If you guessed somewhere between 1,500 and 10,000 feathers per parrot (depending on size and species), you might win something. If you're too busy crying to play, you can cheer yourself up by feeling grateful you don't share your home with a swan. Swans have 25,000 feathers per bird. If you are good at math, you can calculate that one swan equals 16 small or eight large parrots. After learning this, you might also discover you actually enjoy sweeping up after one parrot (small or large) because you realize the other seven or seventeen are molting out their feathers in somebody else's home.

When all else fails, try imagining you are the Dalai Lama. Think how he would react to a seemingly endless cascade of falling feathers. "Feathers fall," he might quip as he smiles brightly and lets out a delighted giggle.

To which your parrot cheeps in reply, fluffs, and releases yet another downy breast feather to join the ever-expanding pile on your living room floor.

<u>Lessons with Wings</u>: *Feathers happen. Thankfully, so do parrots. When I look at my molting parrot, I see nature's protective influence at work keeping Pearl healthy, strong, and safe. In fact, I think we make a pretty good team—nature and me.*

The Tall Tree

It is 8 p.m. My bird is screaming like a two-year-old up way past his bedtime.

And I am on the phone with my mom, explaining that grandparents have responsibilities, regardless of whether the grandchild in question happens to be mammalian or avian.

My dad makes Mom put the call on speakerphone and suggests I have a relaxing glass of wine to calm down. I've already had two, and as soon as I locate the part of me that cares, I am going to give her a stern talking-to about her consumption levels of late.

The problem is, we have just moved. I love our modern and spacious new pad, but Pearl isn't so sure yet. He misses his old familiar haunts in the more rustic space we have left behind, and most especially he is pining for the shiny birdie in the vanity mirror in our old bathroom, with whom he had established a, er, bond.

It is now dawning on Pearl that this particular furnishing did not make the journey with us, and he is frantic. I, too, am frantic, which is making my parents frantic, and the fact that I nearly garroted my featherweight companion in his own cage door by mistake earlier this afternoon is not helping. "Pearl is having such a bad day!" I wail to Mom. "No, YOU are having a bad day," she calmly replies. "Pearl is doing just fine."

Spoken with the weight of truth, as one would expect from a mother to two and now grandmother to four (three small humans and one small parrot). "Why don't you come for dinner tomorrow night—I'll make pizza and Dad will open a bottle of wine." "You know who I'm bringing with me," I warn her. "Bring him," Mom replies. "He can hang out with Dad and calm down."

She means so I can calm down. But Pearl does love his grandfather, aka Dad, aka the "Tall Tree" (a reference both to his 6' 3" in height, and the fact that he often dresses in green) and Mom did mention two staples of my diet—pizza and wine. My dad buys only the finest Franciscan—for the price of one bottle, I could buy a whole caseload of the crap I can usually afford to drink. Plus there is literally nothing cuter than watching Pearl enthusiastically burrow his tiny curved beak into the middle of a huge and delicious slice of piping hot homemade pizza that somebody else was just about to consume. (My mother is a gourmet chef. She swears we saw Julia Child filming live in the Dillard's cooking department when I was a child. To date there is no evidence of this—or any of my mom's culinary DNA—in my limited cooking repertoire.)

When Pearl was five years old, I moved into a house with a roommate where the situation was decidedly inhospitable to avians. I made the decision it would be best if Pearl stayed with the Tall Tree and the Small Tree for a while, at least until I decided if I would continue to live in the new situation long-term and could then bring him over more easily.

Grandparents to the core, Dad was a particular pushover, placidly allowing Pearl to chew through newspapers and library book pages by day and to watch television for hours from the comfort of his knee by night. This indulgence continued for three years with predictable results—to this day, whenever he sees the Tall Tree, Pearl launches himself at him, arching his back, half-spreading his wings, leaning forward like an Olympic sprinter about to spring from the starting block. While visiting, there have been many occasions when Dad and I have left the house to pick up some essential ingredient my mom has needed to complete her latest five-star recipe, not realizing until we arrive back home again that Dad has been wearing the poopy bird towel (this to help Pearl maintain a firm grip as well as to catch certain, um, events) slung across his shoulders during the entire trip.

Not that either of us especially cares. In our households, after all, it is all—and always—about the bird.

<u>Lessons with Wings</u>: *If I commit to care for another being, human or non-human, I also commit to asking for support from others when I need it. While I am typically able to take care of the majority of what Pearl needs on my own, I also have a small group of folks who are always "on call" to help if help is needed.*

Happy

My Big Fat Greek Wedding is a longstanding cinematic favorite here at Casa Feathers n Beak. Pearl likes the festive Greek soundtrack (simply put, bouzouki music rocks) and I like pretty much everything else.

My favorite scene unfolds outside the kitchen at Dancing Zorba's, the Portokalos family restaurant. In this particular scene our heroine, 30-year-old "seating hostess" Fotoula "Toula" Portokalos, sits forlornly atop a stack of packing boxes. She is spending her break staring at a crumpled-up community college brochure describing the computer classes she dreams of taking. At this point we hear her voice narrating, "I wish I had a different life. I wish I was braver. And prettier. Or just happy."

Luckily for Toula, her mom convinces her dad to let her take the longed-for computer classes and her life starts looking up. Similarly, right around the start of my own 30th year, two important mentors arrived to help me change my life trajectory. Mentor number one, Lynn, was my boss at two different jobs, where she excelled at both and I spent a lot of time standing in front of the break room soda machines pounding on the Plexiglas to get my stolen quarters back. Lynn taught me it is okay to want to live, even if you have no idea how and aren't at all sure you can learn. She also taught me that once you admit you want to live, it is then perfectly okay to fight like a dog for your life.

Mentor number two presented as a bit of a bait-and-switch initially, since in those first few weeks of formula feeding, poop cleanup, and 4:30 p.m. bedtimes, I was understandably confused about who was serving whom. But as one of us molted and the other grew up, I realized I had received exactly what I had been asking for all those years: "pretty, brave, and happy," all in one fluffy chick-sized package.

12 years later and counting, Pearl continues to teach me every day that if I want to see something good in myself or my life, my default assumption needs to be that I do have it rather than that I don't. In other words, if I am not at least willing to believe I am brave or pretty, I won't see those qualities in myself even if they are there. Similarly, if I don't train myself to pay attention to the happy moments I have in my daily life—however tiny or fleeting they may be—I will miss my chance to make that happiness grow.

Unlike me, Pearl never misses a chance to celebrate his own beauty, bravery, and happiness. But he doesn't do this out of insecurity or arrogance. Rather, witnessing his sheer childlike delight at discovering that beautiful cockatiel in the mirror once again is rather like watching someone you cherish unexpectedly winning the lottery multiple times. It couldn't be cooler even if it was happening to you (well, maybe a tiny bit cooler, but you'll take it just the same).

In the last several years, the emerging field of "social connectivity" has been studying how our social networks influence our lives. Researchers in this field can now prove that the beings we spend the most time with deeply influence our personality, preferences, life outlook, wellbeing, habits, and more. In other words, we become very much like the closest company we keep.

Since these researchers say nothing about whether or not this social influence factor is limited to human-to-human interactions, I choose to believe it isn't (as proof, I submit that I get reliably happier every single morning in the instant I uncover Pearl's cage and see his sweet little face and hear his cute good morning chirps). And while I vastly prefer Pearl whenever possible, in a pinch the sight of any avian freewheeling above me in the breezes, munching on seed at a feeder, enjoying a fresh rainwater bath, or other similar feathery sightings can produce a feeling of connectedness and joy within me even on the bleakest of days...and even when nothing else can accomplish the same.

In one of my all-time favorite books, *Connected: the Surprising Power of Our Social Networks and How They Shape Our Lives* by Nicholas Christakis and James Fowler, the authors share the results of a survey they conducted with more than 3,000 randomly chosen folks. Data analysis revealed most survey respondents claimed to have just four close social contacts, with a high of eight contacts and a low of no contacts (for survey purposes, contact categories included friends, spouses, family members, mentors, bosses, pastors, and similar others). I personally have nearly 4,000 Facebook "friends" as of the exact moment I am typing this sentence. Yet I can also count on exactly five fingers the number of beings (people and parrots) I immediately reconnected with after a recent extended trip out of town.

This data, as you might imagine, has also been helpful in eradicating lingering angst over never being a member of any "popular crowd." Through reading *Connected* and other books, talking with mentors, and simply growing up, I have slowly but surely realized none of us is "popular"—really. Some of us may serve in roles within our social networks requiring us to make a greater number of more superficial connections in service to sustaining the network and its connections to other networks. But none of us—truly—can maintain more than approximately 12 close social connections at one time without stretching our interpersonal resources to the max. If we have two close contacts, we are well within the societal norms of today.

If we have four or more close contacts, we are richly blessed beyond measure (even more so if one of them has wings).

<u>Lessons with Wings</u>: *If I want to feel prettier, braver, or just happy, the absolute best way to get there is to choose my company carefully. One self-confident, self-loving being (human or non-human) can do more to transform my self-image than an infinite number of casual social acquaintances or social media "friends."*

Potential

Some people like to watch humans or calves being born. I assume this is just because they have never witnessed the miracle of parrot birth.

First, the featherless, blind baby chooses of its own free will to hack its way out of a small but comfortable enclosure that already contains nourishment, shelter, and a handy disguise. The moment the exit maneuver is complete, the baby opens up its mouth to ask its parents for free handouts—which then becomes its sole hobby for about the next month...unless you count pooping and napping.

Around day eight or nine, another miracle occurs—the tiny parrot's eyes open. Now instead of standing still with its beak open, the baby can follow its mom around with its beak open (at which point she likely begins to wonder what the heck she was thinking to have an egg).

Day 10 or 11 brings the first signs of the pin shafts that will eventually cover the baby's pink naked body with feathers and deliver a lifetime of preening, molting, and vacuuming enjoyment for parrot and parront alike.

From this point forward, the no longer tiny but still small parrot baby will learn to walk, to groom, to eat for itself, and—eventually—to figure out what those large folding appendages on either side of its body can do.

Talk about potential.

One of my favorite animal books is *Animals Make Us Human* by Dr. Temple Grandin. Truthfully, I have lots of favorite animal books but I like this one's title the best. We aren't necessarily born wonderful—at least in my opinion. But we are born with the potential to be wonderful. Caring for another creature, especially a dependent baby creature, turns all that pent-up potential into actual tangible wonderfulness.

Whenever I want to know how loving, how kind, how forgiving, how strong, how courageous, how creative, how delightful, how connected, how loving I have the potential to be, all I have to do to find my answer is to look at Pearl.

There is my answer. His whole life—and ours together—is my answer.

What a Bird Wants

"Pearl, wait for Mommy, please. Wait for MOMMY. WAIT for Mommy. *PEARL......*!"

Avian body language isn't subtle. Ever. Wings out, neck hyper-extended (think ostrich, not parrot), dark eyes wide, and individual feathers fairly quivering with anticipation, it is crystal clear Pearl has no intention of waiting for his Mommy's assistance. As usual.

I have to marvel a bit as I watch my bird racing across the bathroom counter, effortlessly sidestepping common perils like toothbrushes, hair gel tubes, and the always problematic oval sink basin—throughout, he keeps his eyes on the goal. Which is, specifically, the blue plastic toiletries basket. He beaks his way up onto the tall blue drinking glass, using it as a launching pad from which to jump across to the edge of the blue basket, and then suddenly (somehow) he is standing in that most magical of spots—both small pink feet perfectly balanced atop the gardenia scented hand cream tube. From there, if he stretches his tiny body up, up, up like so, he can just make out the face of the most beautiful grey and white cockatiel in the large over-the-sink mirror.

Like Sir Edmund Hillary upon reaching the peak of Mount Everest, Pearl reverently soaks in the view—meanwhile, I am not sure whether to applaud or attempt to sneak away (in hopes of conducting at least one shriek-free business phone call while he presides over yet another spontaneous self-admiration society meeting). But the moment my large featherless form disappears past the edge of the crown molding, the warning siren goes off.

Apparently self-admiration society meetings aren't nearly so enjoyable when you are the only attendee.

Phone call forgotten, I return to attend to the inevitable business at hand—assisting my avian with the dismount. Here, again, Pearl has failed to grasp the meaning of the word "wait." When I reach him, he has one foot still gripping the hand cream tube and the other extended out into thin air as he reaches his beak towards the side of the blue basket. This, as always, is a bold maneuver that is destined to fail. I scoop him up with both hands and plant several proud parrontal kisses on top of his brave feathery head.

After all, one of us has to climb Everest. It certainly isn't going to be me.

<u>Lessons with Wings</u>: *If there is one quality that parrots possess in spades, it is courage. If something happens that they don't prefer (vet visit, hawk sighting) they protest their involvement with the vigor of a thousand parrots. If a delicacy or favorite toy is proffered (whether it is meant for them or not) they jump on top of it without hesitation to stake their claim. Whatever Pearl wants, he goes for it 150 percent. With his help, I hope to one day look back upon my life and see the same.*

Parrot in the HOUSE

I have a friend who loves to throw parties. He particularly enjoys greeting arriving guests by announcing their name and then adding "in the HOUSE!"

For example, when I arrive I can expect to hear a strenuously enthusiastic, "Shannon Cutts in the HOUSE!" For fellow extroverts, this greeting is enlivening. For introverts like me, the effect is not unlike the lingering trauma that occurs when you are out shopping and the intercom system comes on to announce there is a certain car in the parking lot with its lights left on...followed by a very public recitation of your license plate number.

With Pearl, however, the challenge is typically more along the lines of getting the host to stop announcing himself long enough to notice actual guests have walked in. In this, Pearl and I are clearly a happy case of "opposites attract."

For instance, when I have guests over I don't have to worry about making conversation. Pearl takes care of that. Similarly, if I want to get off the phone quickly, all I have to do is stand near Pearl's cage, phone in hand, and wait for him to notice and start screeching (a phone-jealous child has nothing on a phone-jealous parrot). As well, cute cockatiel stories always make for great icebreakers (especially if your fellow nervous stranger also has pets...or kids). Finally, nothing eases interpersonal tension like exclaiming, "Pearl! No pooping!," in the middle of a heated conversation.

I have also noticed that since Pearl automatically assumes everyone else will like him as much as a) he likes himself and, b) his Mommy likes him, it nearly always works out that they do. As such, presenting a Pearl-first face to a grumpy landlord, neighbor, boyfriend, or best friend can offer certain strategic advantages. In fact, even if you don't have a pet, you can still test this out by bringing a picture of a cute puppy to your next big negotiation. When it comes time to deliver the verdict, make the deciding party stare at the puppy while they answer.

It is hard to say no to a very cute puppy. Or a very cute parrot.

<u>Lessons with Wings</u>: *For many years, mentors have told me that how I face the world is how the world faces me. But Pearl doesn't bother with telling—he just lives out this truth right in front of me. Pearl faces the world with the expectation he will be accepted, liked, included, and nurtured. As I strive to follow his lead, the world is slowly but surely becoming a much friendlier, more welcoming place.*

Wesley and Stacey and Pearl and Me

When Wesley opened his tiny owlet eyes for the very first time, Stacey O'Brien's warm and welcoming ones were right there to meet his.

From that moment forward, he was hooked. If Stacey left his direct line of sight—even for a moment—Wesley would shriek loudly enough to deafen the entire owl biology lab at Caltech. Stacey, then a 20-something junior researcher working in the Caltech lab, had just agreed to take on an unprecedented long-term research project, one never before attempted in the history of barn owl studies.

The owlet was rescued in the woods by some hikers who, luckily for Wesley, were smart enough to bring him to Caltech right away for evaluation. As it turned out, Wesley had nerve damage in his wing and because of this, he would never be able to survive if released back into the wild. Since the owlet's eyes had not yet opened, Caltech staff realized the baby's unique circumstances represented a priceless opportunity to both save a baby owl and at the same time further their research. They wanted to see what would happen if the owlet was allowed to imprint on (or bond with) a caring human mama—preferably one who was also trained to research and document owl behavior.

When asked if she was willing, Stacey says it took her all of two seconds to say "Yes! Yes!" to a project that would absolutely consume the next 20 years of her life. From that moment forward, Wesley and Stacey began a relationship that would end up saving them both.

The early years presented some unusual challenges. For instance, what exactly was the protocol for a single owlet Mama to accept dinner dates when the third member of the dinner party required that raw mouse parts be hand-fed to him at regular intervals throughout the meal? The correct protocol, as it turned out, was no dinner dates—a constraint Stacey readily accepted for Wesley's sake during their 19 years together.

Not that Stacey lacked for companionship. During Wesley's baby years, he cuddled with his mom as much as any owlet would. As he matured, Wesley's interest in Stacey shifted, and he chose her as his mate. This presented yet another challenging hurdle for Stacey to overcome. A mated owl in the wild is extremely attentive to even the smallest aspects of their mate's wellbeing, paying close attention to ensure their beloved is getting enough rest, grooming, attention, and…nutrition. From that point forward, Stacey had to pretend to eat a raw dead mouse at least once each day or Wesley would get very upset.

Once again, Stacey made it work for Wesley's sake. Then Stacey fell ill—very ill. She was diagnosed with a brain tumor that turned her life completely upside down.

Everything changed, and not for the better. Of this time in her life, she shares:

I went to a very dark place…but I realized I couldn't abandon Wesley. He was so emotional and so deeply attached to me. He got me through that hard time. And through that I really learned with my heart that it's enough just to have the ability to love. The things we use to define ourselves are false. The only thing that really matters is—we are capable of giving love. That's why we are on this planet.

In so many ways Stacey and Wesley's story is my own and Pearl's as well. Both Wesley and Pearl had wing damage that rendered them unusually dependent on humans for care and support. Both Stacey and I battled a serious, potentially life-limiting (even life-ending) health issue. In each of our cases, when our winged mates needed us, we eagerly rose to the occasion. And when we needed them, they offered us the same and so much more.

I love Stacey's words: "The things we use to define ourselves are false. The only thing that really matters is—we are capable of giving love. That's why we are on this planet."

If Pearl has taught me anything (and he has taught me so much) it is that Stacey's words ring true. Nothing else but love really matters.

NOTHING.

You can connect with Stacey and celebrate Wesley's life by visiting her at: **www.wesleytheowl.com**

<u>Lessons with Wings</u>: *Stacey's words say it all. From the moment I met Pearl I called him "love with wings." More than a decade later, he continues to administer daily life-saving doses of pure love to me—and to receive the same from me in return.*

On the Subject of Who is Prettiest

This morning I took one look at the bright, sunny, cloudless sky and 102-degree thermometer reading and promptly began rummaging around in my drawers for the oldest, yuckiest workout clothes I could find.

Locating a once-white ragged t-shirt and some equally unattractive mustard yellow jogging shorts, I knotted my hair back, slipped on a pair of ancient mud-encrusted tennis shoes and enthusiastically set off for the gravel exercise trail located a few minutes from my house.

I had been walking vigorously for about half a mile and was already dripping with sweat when a white SUV traveling past suddenly swerved into the parking lane and then jerked to a stop right across the street from me. The driver-side door opened and a solidly built young Middle Eastern-looking guy with short black hair and a white long-sleeved dress shirt jumped out. He was clutching a small silver cell phone. He also looked a bit wild in the eyes as he turned about, zeroed in on me, and strode over. Taking into account the sudden stop, the cell phone, the nervous energy, and the fact that I was the lone visible walker on a two-mile community trail, I naturally assumed he was lost.

"Hi. I was driving by and couldn't help but notice." I pasted what I hoped was an understanding smile on my face—I get lost frequently, too—and waited. "My name is Brian and you are very beautiful and I was wondering if you would like to get coffee sometime soon."

Okay. So clearly not lost then. "Oh. Well, thanks so much, but I have a boyfriend." (This is not precisely the truth, but there is a guy I've been seeing, and now doesn't seem the ideal moment to attempt to work out the social niceties of explaining to your already-not-yet-boyfriend about your new-not-yet-boyfriend that you are meeting for coffee later.) "The prettiest ones always do," Brian sighed. I smiled and proffered a lame, "Well, nice to meet you, um—thanks for..." and I gestured to my sweat-soaked person and laughed. Brian gave me one last lingering look up and down and replied, "Oh, you have nothing to apologize for. Believe me, it is much sexier than you know." Then he waved goodbye and jumped back into his SUV—a swarthy young James Bond on a hormonally charged mission to find a last-minute mid-afternoon coffee date.

This was not as strange an experience as I might wish it were. In fact, I have actually lost count of the number of times I have been waylaid in similar fashion at grocery stores, in parking lots, during thunderstorms at the local park, and now on the neighborhood exercise trail. The sole common denominator? On each occasion I have been literally marinating in my own sweat.

The ultimate irony here is that when I am wearing my most alluring new outfit, high posterior-shaping platform heels, makeup perfect, and hair fresh from the styling salon, the men stay away. In fact, I can almost sense them there, forming a loose, slightly menacing competitive ring around my pristine personal periphery. They are waiting...waiting...waiting...for that very first drop of pheromone-laced sweat to fall. This is their cue to rush in.

While I am still trying to get used to this phenomenon, my bird was born ready. For more than 12 years now I have been waking Pearl up in the morning. And for more than 12 years now, the moment his cage cover comes off, the exact same routine unfolds. First, he scampers out. Next, he locates the nearest reflective surface. At this point, I hear a loud and appreciative avian wolf whistle—or several. Pearl has spied his own reflection and is reliably delighted with what he sees. In the moment Pearl encounters a mirror, he can be fresh from a shower, feathers bedraggled and dripping, in mid-molt with spiky pin feathers ringing his neck like a medieval monarch's cape, or in full feather and looking mighty fine indeed, but his reaction is always the same: "Oh! Pretty!! VERY pretty!! Pretty, PRETTY birdie!!!"

Here I admit I cannot recall a time when I have ever had this reaction to the sight of myself first thing in the morning...or at any time of day, to be honest. This is also why I always ask participants in my speaking programs to raise their hands if they have a pet. For those who don't, their homework assignment is to get one. Pets are great for modeling healthy self-esteem.

And for pretty much everything else, come to think of it.

<u>Lessons with Wings</u>: *While neither Pearl nor I will ever think I am prettier than he is, the prettiest bird in the whole world (by his own admission) has miraculously chosen to spend his life with me. To Pearl I am his mommy, his mate, his entire flock. If I am pretty enough for Pearl, well, that is pretty enough for me!*

For the Love of a Parrot

A casual internet search on the phrase "for the love of a woman" turns up no fewer than a dozen Google hits—and that is just for song lyrics and only on page one.

A similar search on "for the love of a parrot" turns up a YouTube video of two parrots dancing to "What is Love," a selection of parrot-related nonprofit organizations, a few bland how-to articles, and one rather aggressively worded blog post about how the writer's parrot is not a pet but a family member for life (for the record, I happen to agree wholeheartedly).

With ever-increasing numbers of folks trading in their human best friends for feathery (or furred or shelled or finned) replacements, I feel it is safe to assume that those of us lucky enough to have both exert ourselves similarly on either species' behalf. In fact, I have often experienced how loving a parrot partner—for better or worse, for richer or poorer, in sickness and in health—is in its own way every bit as challenging and rewarding as loving a human partner.

For instance, as a parront, I am no longer free to simply come and go as I please. I have responsibilities and they are not optional. When I am home, each day's required agenda includes feeding and watering and cage changing and sweeping and neck feather scratching and all the rest. When I am away from home it is necessary to make sure someone I trust takes care of each of these needs for Pearl.

In the same way, as a parront, I receive unconditional love and companionship from my parrot. Pearl trusts me implicitly—sometimes I suspect he trusts me more than I trust me. He also wants me around all the time—even when I am in such a bad mood I don't want myself around.

In loving Pearl, sometimes I also see things about myself I don't like. Selfishness, laziness, pettiness—thanks to my relationship with Pearl I now know I possess all of these unattractive traits (and plenty more where they came from). But because I love Pearl and he loves me back and depends on me for everything, I can't just give up on myself when I see something within me I don't like. I have to work on it, change what needs changing, and continue to show up for myself and for Pearl during it all.

Otherwise I risk losing that most precious of life's gifts—the chance to grow into my full potential in the presence of a being who already loves me exactly the way I am.

<u>Lessons with Wings</u>: *I love those stickers that say "Dear God, may I be the person my dog thinks I am." In my mind I just substitute "parrot"—and then proceed to strive towards that oh-so-worthy goal for another day.*

Beak to Beak

Several years ago Pearl became inexplicably restless. No matter what I tried it didn't work to calm him down.

Ever the concerned parront, I promptly called my friend Ray, bird breeder extraordinaire, and made a reservation for Pearl at Ray's posh birdie hotel. I figured a few days in the company of those for whom chirping was a first language should set him to rights again. While Pearl was away, I had an early mid-life crisis and decided to get my nose pierced. I had always admired the sparkly noses of the Indian women I had met years earlier in Mumbai. I guess I just needed about an extra decade (and perhaps an adult beverage or two) to work up the courage to try the look for myself.

Pearl was enjoying himself so much at the birdie hotel he stayed on for a couple extra weeks, during which time my new piercing continued to heal up nicely. I had chosen a small shiny diamante for my left nostril and I enjoyed admiring it every time I passed by a mirror. The day finally came to pick up my feathery guy, and I could hear him shrieking for me the moment my tires rolled across Ray's driveway. Pearl scrambled out of his cage and up onto my finger—rarely had he seemed so overjoyed to see me.

As it turned out, reunion wasn't the only thing on his mind. The moment he got close enough, he reached out his sharp little curved beak and nipped that shiny diamante right out of my still-sensitive healing nose. Shoving the mangled remains back in, I hurriedly plunked Pearl into his cage, waved goodbye to Ray, and rushed home to survey the damage. $75 and a course of antibiotics later (along with a stern lecture from my doc about how the 20s and not the 30s were the appropriate years for ideas like nose piercings) I officially retired what was left of the diamante to my mementos chest.

Not having Pearl around for a few weeks had helped me forget why parronts as a rule tend to forgo jewelry. Simply put, birds like shiny things—a lot. There is little more painfully memorable than ringside seats for yet another round of nostril (or earlobe, or finger) versus beak. In my personal experience thus far, the parrontal appendage always loses...and its owner adds a trip to the jewelry repair store and possibly the family physician to their to-do list. For this very reason, Pearl now has his own selection of "jewelry"—avian-safe, inexpensive strings of odds and ends he can boss around, dismantle, and otherwise rearrange at will.

I have also gotten relatively skilled at explaining away the selection of small scrapes and scratches my nose tends to collect whenever it comes in range of a certain diminutive hooked beak. In the early years, I thought Pearl was being aggressive. But now I know better, thanks entirely to a documentary film called *The Wild Parrots of Telegraph Hill* (see "Me and Mark Bittner" to learn more). The story features the antics of a small flock of green conures that frequents San Francisco's famed Telegraph Hill. "Beak grabbing"—a practice in which one bird grips and shakes the beak of another for the purpose of receiving the gift of regurgitated food (yum)—is common both in courtship and rearing of the young. In fact, young birds that are perfectly capable of feeding themselves often continue to follow their parents around for months after leaving the nest, begging for free beak handouts.

One day not long after I saw the film, I glimpsed myself in the mirror at a moment when my lips made contact with Pearl's soft feathery midsection yet again. In that instant, it occurred to me that whenever I kiss Pearl's belly, his beak and my nose are nearly parallel. Having formula fed him from the time he was a chick, I am officially "mom."

So it just makes sense that as a hungry adult bird he might still from time to time reach out to grasp my "beak," hoping for a tasty handout as any savvy chick would.

<u>Lessons with Wings</u>: *I love to read. If the subject matter happens to be about birds (parrots in particular) even better. In recent years I have discovered a literal wealth of bird literature to explain behaviors I have in the past tended to a) disregard, b) make up a reason for or, c) worry about. I am also (happily) finding out that the more informed I choose to be, the healthier and more mutually respectful my connection with Pearl becomes. Some might say lucky Pearl for having a parront who is willing to learn. I say lucky me for having a parrot who is willing to teach!*

Me by Me

I have always wanted to write a book. From the time I was a small girl I read voraciously.

When I was eight I even won a contest sponsored by our local paper for reading the most books in one summer (this must have been the summer I had no friends). I was also a spelling bee champ, and I reveled in the ease with which I mastered the English language, English writing assignments, and anything else that didn't fall under the category of "cooking," "sports," "science," or "math."

In 2009 I finally managed to write a whole book—and get it published, too. Health Communications, Inc., did the honors when they bought *Beating Ana: How to Outsmart Your Eating Disorder and Take Your Life Back,* a book that describes in detail how peer mentoring can work to support people recovering from eating disorders. It has since sold at least 25 copies, and my mom has finally stopped asking, "Who is Ana and why are they beating her?" ("ana" = anorexia). But even though at long last I met my goal of becoming a published author, it still isn't enough.

I know this because of a little paperback I recently discovered in my parents' attic called *Me by Me: My Own Book.* While I didn't choose the compelling title of this fill-in-the-blanks kids' book, my second grade self apparently wasted no time filling in its pages with choice nuggets of youthful aspiration, inspiration, and wisdom. For instance:

It hurt the most when I "broke a muscle."
The best day of my life in school was "when I won the spelling bee."

The worst day of my life in school was "when I made an F on my math."
If I had a million dollars I would "do everything."

Even more revealing, however, were these gems:

The world record I would like to set is "most birds."
When I grow up I will "raise birds."
The world will "buy my birds."
Remember these famous words of mine: "I love birds."

To date, no one I know has bought any of my birds. This might be because I don't have any birds for sale.

It is also worth noting I don't have any plans to raise or sell any birds—at least not until my houseplants and fish stop dying way ahead of schedule. And if anyone tries to buy or otherwise remove Pearl from the premises...well, let's just say I still remember a few of those moves from my college karate class and I'm not afraid to use them.

So this book appears to be yet another lifelong dream coming true. I always assumed being in the midst of my own dream coming true would be more relaxing and less stressful than it is, but that just shows how much the kid-me knew about anything the adult-me might later encounter. Truthfully, it is a bit (okay quite) nerve-wracking to watch myself, typing away on my laptop long after Pearl has retired for the night, writing about him and me and us and the little girl who wanted to be remembered for nothing more nor less than saying, "I love birds."

Which I do. I really, truly do.

<u>Lessons with Wings</u>: *My childhood dreams are still my dreams today. I wanted my life to be full of birds (or at least bird). I wanted to be happy...to be able to focus on what I do well and leave the rest to more capable others...to love...to "do everything." And I still want all of these things.*

Paint Your Pet

When I was in my twenties, I was finally beginning to catch glimpses of light at the end of the long tunnel of battling an eating disorder.

So I did what any self-respecting 20-something who narrowly averts death and is very proud of herself would do—I went off to India to look for God.

I am not sure now why I thought God would be there. But since it seemed like so many other people who were looking for God started their search in India, and I had never been there before, and I love to travel, and traveling in India is cheap for people like me who never seem to have much money, India it was. Plus a humanitarian organization I was volunteering with at the time had an opening for a long-term staff volunteer who was willing to travel to India and had no special skills. I was a perfect fit.

While I was in India, I heard a story about a man who owned a goat. The man was a farmer and he didn't have much money either but he wanted to find God very badly. He went to a local guru (that is Indian for "teacher") and he begged the guru to teach him how to find God. The guru gave him all sorts of instructions about sitting for meditation, posture, breathing, mantras, and more. The man went home, went over all the instructions again in his mind, sat down and got comfy and did each thing in its proper order and then waited for his big experience. Then his nose started to itch. He sneezed. The goat got hungry and head-butted him (I could really relate to this one).

So the man went back to the guru. He was upset because the instructions weren't working and he felt very defeated. The guru gave him some new instructions and sent him back home again. Again, the man sat down, got comfy, reviewed the new instructions in his mind, and tried to meditate to find God. Again, nothing happened. This time when the man went back to see the guru he was convinced there was no hope for him. He was quite distraught. The guru said to the man, "What do you love the most?" The man answered, "I love my goat the most." The guru then instructed him to return home and meditate on his goat. The guru said to him, "I want you to think of every single thing you love about your goat—his fuzzy coat, his soft black eyes, his cute little bleating sounds."

The man was delighted. Now THIS he could do. He hurried right back home, eager to begin. Starting that very afternoon, the farmer sat down every day at the same time and began to meditate on his love for his goat. He went into great detail in his visualizations of the goat's adorable small feet, his diminutive furry ears, the gentle wheezing sounds he made when he was asleep. Little by little, the man's heart began to open more and more. He was so busy—and so happy—meditating on his goat he didn't even realize it when, at long last, God exploded in his heart and he became one with everything.

The moral of this story—for me at least—is that it is perfectly okay to love your pet to distraction. Unfortunately, I didn't hear the story until I had already bought my $1,000 ticket to Mumbai (so not quite so cheap as I was hoping for, it turned out) and spent six months not shaving and wearing pajamas out in public. Don't get me wrong—to this day I treasure my experiences in India and wouldn't trade them for anything. But I didn't find God in India. I found God right where I left (him? her?) back at home during a rousing session of "Paint Your Pet" on my mom's birthday a couple of years ago.

Here is what happened. Every year like clockwork, my mom has another birthday. And every year like clockwork, my dad panics about what to get her for her present. Sometimes Mom throws out helpful clues my dad doesn't catch, like talking for days on end about the precious painting the next door neighbor just did of her dog, Mr. Nippers, in a class called "Paint Your Pet."

This particular year, being the sensitive, savvy person I am, I once again picked up on her unsubtle hints and suggested to my dad that he spring for two birthday tickets to the class (I would need to go along, of course, just to make sure Mom had the best time possible). Dad jumped at the idea. A few minutes later, Mom and I were signed up for the very next session of "Paint Your Pet."

Before our class date, I had to send in pictures of J.P. Morgan, my parents' extra-long brown dachshund, and Pearl. The "Paint Your Pet" people were very excited about the student who would be painting the bird—apparently not too many people sign up to paint birds. This is probably because birds are very small and hard to paint even for expert painters (I am not in this category), but of course I wouldn't find that out for a couple of weeks yet.

Luckily, by the time I did find this out, I had also discovered the painting place was BYOB and arranged for appropriate libations to help the creative process along. When Mom and I arrived for our class, we discovered the instructors had cleverly blown up our tiny 4X6 full color pet photos into portrait-sized gray scale "paint by numbers" reproductions. We would be expected to correctly identify and color in our own pets' predominant colors ("brown" and "grey," respectively) but the instructors would be on hand throughout to offer assistance with such delicate subtleties as which cup is for wine and which cup is for washing out our paintbrushes.

We spent the next approximately two hours wielding paintbrushes like experts while wearing aprons that looked like victims of a mass Monet drive-by, all the while drinking expensive wine, eating delectable snacks, and meditating on our pets.

I took my time and studied in great detail the way Pearl cocks his sweet little bird head, how bright and intelligent his soft round black eyes are, how brave he is to cope with his damaged left wing without complaint or self-pity, the amazing strength and tenacity of his tiny and mostly clawless pink feet, his cute little hooked beak, the delicate curve of his feathery crest...until all of a sudden I realized God has had wings all along.

186

<u>**Lessons with Wings**</u>: *God is love. Period, the end. So if I want to have a relationship with God, I must seek first and only this—a relationship with love.*

Not an Ostrich

Pearl and I enjoy watching movies together.

While often my enjoyment focuses more on the plot and soundtrack and his enjoyment focuses more on the reflective quality of the television screen and the interesting crunchy-chewy texture of the DVD box, there are a few favorite flicks that are compelling enough to align our shared interests in favor of the former.

One such film is the animated bird-centric classic, *Rio*. The plot centers on a pair of characters that could be our on-screen doubles: Blu, a blue macaw, and his parront, a book-loving single gal named Linda. As the film begins, Blu and Linda are spending their days in contented solitude tending the counter together at "Blue Macaw Books," Linda's small bookshop in icy rural Minnesota.

Linda and Blu had first met many years previously when a bird smuggling van trundled through the town, hit a bump, and unknowingly ejected a single cage containing the tiny blue captured chick out into the snow. Linda rescued Blu and took him in, and the rest, as it were, was history.

At least until Tulio, an ornithologist from Brazil, comes calling. Tulio has an urgent mission only Blu can fulfill. Before they realize what is happening, Linda and Blu are en route to the tropics so Blu can meet Jewel, the last known female blue macaw in existence. His mission? To make more baby blue macaws to carry on the species.

As with every coming-of-age story, along the way Blu is called upon to come out of his shell, so to speak, and address a variety of hang-ups, fears, and misconceptions.

One of Blu's primary hang-ups is an inexplicable inability to fly. As the film progresses it becomes clear the hapless yet highly intelligent blue parrot has developed a variety of coping mechanisms, including everything from humor to rationalization, to explain away his handicap. In one scene he points out to Jewel—a flight-loving bird if ever there was one—that there are lots of birds who can't fly, including the ostrich. "You are NOT an ostrich!" she snaps in utter frustration.

Then they meet Rafael. Rafael, a toucan saddled with an overbearing wife and 18 rambunctious chicks, sees in Blu and Jewel just the refreshing adventure his unrelenting parenting schedule has ordered. Together, they set out for Rio to see what can be done about the worldwide blue macaw shortage. In the interests of the mission, Rafael also decides Blu is long overdue for a flying lesson. Using a combination of positive peer pressure, scientific fact, practical instruction, encouragement, matchmaking, and mentoring, he reassures Blu that flying is in his DNA. As he explains to Blu, "Flying is not what you think up here [points to head], it's what you feel in here [thumps chest]. And when you feel the rhythm of your heart, you FLY!"

Predictably, it takes Blu several more bumbling misadventures before he manages to locate the "rhythm of your heart" within his own feathered chest and finally achieves lift-off.

In the same way, for so many years I searched for reasons—excuses—any explanation at all for why I was "the way that I was." Through battling an eating disorder and depression and for other reasons besides, I found myself to be lacking in so many areas that over time I actually sectioned myself off into tiny little compartments, pulling out only this or that aspect as the occasion might call for it, but taking care never to show the whole (and I was sure horrifying) me to anyone. In social situations in particular, I would first study my conversation mates and then I would consult my inner "me inventory" to determine which parts of me I thought companion A or B might find acceptable or entertaining or both. Then, while interacting, I would be sure to reveal only those parts and not one iota more. In this way, I became an arguably lovable, always welcome, even quite funny, yet still totally flightless ostrich.

It took choosing to share my life with a truly flightless bird whose self-esteem could run circles around mine to realize I might just be hiding away the best parts of me. For as long as I've known him, Pearl's attitude has always been, "So I can't fly—check out this other cool thing I can do!" In fact, his damaged left wing has given him the sweetest personality of any bird I have ever known as well as a creative, inventive nature that even manages to turn flightlessness into an enviable asset. I have always admired beings who cope with their weaknesses by reframing them as strengths. Pearl does this effortlessly. But until I met him, I did not know it was possible for me to do the same.

If Pearl and I had concealed our "inner ostriches" from each other when we first met—for him, his desperate need for a way to escape his bullying nest mates, and for me, my need for a lifeline to escape my grief over my cockatiel Jacob's death—we would not be together today.

Luckily, something within each of us gave us the courage to open up, admit our need for each other, and connect. Because of this, today we are both learning to "fly"...together.

<u>Lessons with Wings</u>: *While I am admittedly more introverted than my feathery sidekick, with his help I have realized that I, too, need to allow myself to be a part of a flock. Today, with the encouragement and love of my flock to support me, I am slowly but surely "finding my wings."*

Animal Mentors

In one of my many other lives, I work in the field of eating disorders recovery. And mentoring. Together.

Earlier I mentioned how, several years ago, I founded a nonprofit organization called MentorCONNECT. We are the first global eating disorders mentoring community. Our mission is to offer free services to pair recovered folks with recovering folks in mentoring partnerships so the recovering folks don't get too discouraged and stop trying to recover. It is hard to argue that recovery (from anything!) is impossible when you have a recovered person repeatedly telling you, "No, it is not impossible—I recovered and I believe you can, too."

Everyone who works at MentorCONNECT, myself included, is a volunteer. It is hard work and over the years I have often thought I must have been crazy to launch such a venture. But mentors saved my life and it just felt right to try to return the favor.

And of course everyone at MentorCONNECT knows all about my bird. In fact, one of the many priceless insights I have gained through working at MentorCONNECT is a growing awareness of just how many people other than me look to their animal companions and to nature for encouragement, courage, love, and support. I love looking at pictures of MentorCONNECT members with their pets for precisely this reason. Some members have very interesting pets, too. While most members have cats or dogs and more than a few have birds, some others have horses, iguanas, rabbits, and one member even has alpacas (think "small furry camel" and you'll get a fairly accurate visual).

While often new MentorCONNECT members are initially pessimistic about things like their overall worthiness as a person and their chances of recovering, all it takes is a mention of their pets and they brighten right up. Before long they are recounting in long form about how loving and loyal their animal companions are. At this point I usually catch myself thinking, "Well, you must be pretty wonderful too if you have such a great pet who wants to hang out with you all day long."

Yet in my personal experience, this understanding does not always come naturally. What I mean by this is, while I tend to automatically feel flattered and honored whenever a choosy human being selects me to be their friend, in the past I have found it somewhat less intuitive to perceive the same when an equally choosy non-human being invites me into their inner circle. The truth is, Pearl may be in a position of having to rely on me for food and shelter, but this in no way obligates him to offer love and friendship in return. He offers these additional gifts because he wants to—same as me.

So today, even as I can see a deliberate, meaningful purpose for the mentors, colleagues, friends, and family members who inhabit my life, I can no longer believe it is any accident Pearl and I have specifically come together while there are so many other cockatiels on this planet I will probably never meet. I know I chose the right parrot for me. And I strive every day to be that parront with such great potential whom Pearl chose more than a decade ago.

On the days I fail, and there continue to be many, my bird jumps in without hesitation or recrimination to mentor me once again in the art of unconditional love, patience, and forgiveness. For instance, some days I might get irked at him for shrieking into the phone receiver when I am actually mad at the person on the other end. Other days I might get uselessly frustrated when he does what comes naturally on my (our) fuzzy light blue bathrobe instead of on his cage paper. But then five minutes later, and at a moment when I would likely still be holding a grudge if our situations were reversed, he is head-butting me to scratch his neck feathers. Loving. Forgiving. Oh-so-patient.

Reminding me I have it in me to offer the same in return.

When I was living in India, the local people shared with me a beautiful belief. They believe that when you gaze into the eyes of a child under the age of two, you look directly into the eyes of God. I have often felt the same when gazing into the eyes of a companion animal who has come under my care.

Each time I look directly into Pearl's soft round black eyes, he mirrors back to me all that is good within me, within him, and between us, and the unending potential of much more of the same still yet to come.

<u>Lessons with Wings</u>: *Often in my life I have found myself holding out for a certain type of love from a certain type of being in order to prove to myself that I was worthy (of what, I now wonder). But today I know it doesn't matter who is doing the loving, or whether that being is animal or human. All that matters is that I am loved—and that I love in return.*

Part Three

Extras! (Even More of Pearl)

Extras!

In this third section you will find extras Pearl and his mommy have selected just for you.

For those of you who like to read the "Photo Section" first (I know I do!) you can dive right into feathery cuteness as soon as you turn this page.

For members of the media, bloggers, fact lovers, and, well, everyone really, prepare to be shocked and amazed while reading "The Power of Pets."

For chefs (aspiring and fully, er, fledged), "Pearl's Favorite Waffle Recipe" gives you a taste of goodness yet to come when we release Pearl's cookbook...soon.

For all those who encouraged and supported us throughout this project, Pearl and I dole out richly deserved kudos in "Thankfuls."

Finally, meet us both and keep in touch in "Author Bios."

Enjoy! ☺

Photo Section

In the pages to follow, you will meet Perky, my first parakeet, his blue and white sidekick, Paulie, and Jacob (my first sweet cockatiel).

You will also get to meet Pearl's Grandpa (the Tall Tree), Pearl's Grandma (the Small Tree), and their exceptionally long standard dachshund, J.P. Morgan.

And, of course, you will meet Pearl….and his doting mommy.

My first parrot, a yellow and green parakeet I named Perky. We were instant soulmates.

Perky. Me.

Hanging out with Paulie, a sweet little blue parakeet who happily played second fiddle to Perky.

Me with Jacob, my first cockatiel. It is still very hard for me to think about his passing—or even to look at pictures of us. Grief is a mysterious, lingering thing.

Oh happy day—the day Pearl became my "forever birdie" and I became his "forever mommy!"

Pearl and I cut up the fresh breakfast strawberries together.

Someone small with
fetching feathers shows off
his "lucky left wing" and
two of the three toes that
are missing claws.

Mommy and her birdie
give each other "welcome
home" kisses.

A rousing game of "Hide n
Seek" in progress....Pearl
is in charge (as usual).

Pearl. Admiring
prettiness.

Looking pretty and plump,
a certain waffle-loving
avian weighs in at a robust
77 grams.

Dr. Fix and Karen the Vet
Tech. And Pearl (who is
executing his patented
series of "V.E.T. evasive
maneuvers").

The Zen Yoga Waffle Hawk
displaying "peaceful fierceness"
(or perhaps "fierce peacefulness")
on his mommy's knee.

The signature style that
launched Wet Bird Couture—
the "Baby Bald Eagle."

Pearl consults with one of
his personal style mentors.

When you are famous and feathery, it is only a matter of time before a slavishly devoted fan (in this case, your mommy) will want to paint your portrait.

"Whenever I look in the mirror....I see something positive." —*sketch of Pearl by a VIP fan*

Pearl samples the crispy cover of his mommy's first book, *Beating Ana: how to outsmart your eating disorder and take your life back.*

Mommy's writing assistant diligently supervises her rent-earning efforts.

Scaling the blue bathroom basket—a favorite daily activity here at Casa Feathers n Beak.

Every manly manbird needs an oh-so-masculine wicker "man-cave basket" to retreat to!

Pearl. Looking fetching and feathery for the ladybirds in his newly acquired Easter (nest) basket.

The fearsome grey and white "Mini Blind Vampire" poses proudly next to a fresh kill.

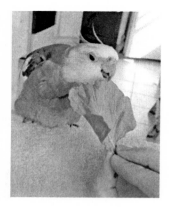

Everything (even
spinach!) tastes better
when it is served
"handfed."

The Greens Gourmand
gets a beak-full of
broccoli's uniquely
aromatic "bouquet."

Someone with feathers
caught in the act of
sampling (yet another)
unauthorized green
household delicacy.

Pasta. It just tastes
better when it's shared.

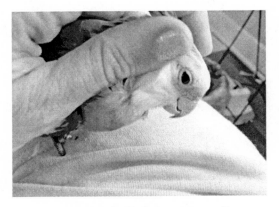

One (1) "neck feathers massage" as
ordered.

The reigning champ in the
Featherweight Division displays award-
winning "Big Wings."

A sole randomly selected, certified objective panelist (with feathers) takes a sample from the "puffy" Cheetos® bag.

The panelist takes a sample from the "crunchy" Cheetos® bag.

Ray and Sarah at the Birdie Hotel.

J.P. Morgan, our family's extra-long
brown standard dachshund, rocking his
favorite raincoat in Provincetown, Cape
Cod. Morgan and I share a birthday, and
he is just one year younger than Pearl.

Pearl occupying his favorite perch on his personal Tall Tree (aka his grandpa, who at 6'3" is the 'approved height' cockatiels prefer).

The Small Tree (aka the Small Chef, aka Grandma) admiring her grandbird up close.

Mommy and her birdie, "beak to beak."

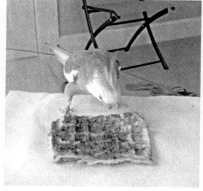

"Sumo" waffle consumption stance—perfect for when you need to guard your waffle and eat it too.

Appendix 1: The Power of Pets

Whether your "pet of choice" is a parrot, a dog, a cat, a turtle, a fish, or something more exotic, the power of pets in our lives today is undeniable...and clearly essential.

Did you know—

- 62 percent of American homes today contain one or more humans and one or more pets. [Nielsen]
- 58 percent of American pet owners call themselves "Mommy" and "Daddy" when referring to their relationship with their pets. [*Psychology Today*]
- 95 percent of Americans consider their pets to be members of the family and 81 percent consider their pets to be *equal* members of the family. [Nielsen]
- Increasing numbers of women in their 20's and 30's are choosing to have a pet over having a child. [*New York Post*]
- An estimated 40 million parrots live in American households today. [Encyclopedia Britannica's *Advocacy for Animals*]
- The African Grey parrot has the emotional intelligence of a two-year-old child and the intellectual intelligence of a five-year-old child. [*Alex & Me*, Dr. Irene Pepperberg]
- Americans spend $5+ billion annually on pet birthday and holiday gifts and outfits—including $350+ million for Halloween costumes and $703+ million for Valentine's Day gifts. [National Retail Federation]
- Pet owners also plunk down $58+ billion annually on pet care products and services for their 397 million pets. [American Pet Products Association]

- On average, people spend just 45 minutes per day with their beloved animal companions, yet they spend more money on their pets than they do on retirement savings or alcohol! [Bureau of Labor Statistics]
- 95 percent of Americans say they smile at least once a day because of their pets. [i-pets]
- The feel-good hormone that keeps pet owners coming back for more is called "oxytocin." Oxytocin supports bonding between a mother and her newborn, cements partner bonds, reduces stress and fear, increases social recognition and generosity, facilitates empathy and trust, and increases feelings of love. [Psych Central]
- The benefits of pet ownership include fewer allergies, lower blood pressure, less anxiety and depression, and fewer cases of heart disease. [WebMD]
- Employees who participate in "bring your dog to work" programs report an up to 11 percent reduction in workday stress. Non-participating employees report an estimated 70 percent increase in workday stress. [*USA Today*]
- People with pets live longer on average than non-pet owners. [Paws for Reaction]
- 40 percent of married dog owners report they receive more emotional support from their pet than from their spouse or kids. [American Animal Hospital Association]
- When asked who they talk to when they get upset, many children (and adults!) say it is their pet. [NIH]
- 38 percent of Americans call home from work to talk to their pet. [PetFinder]
- 20 percent of survey respondents stated they prefer to spend time with their pet rather than spending time with other human beings (this increases to 30 percent for introverts and those who live in more rural areas). [Public Policy Poll]
- More than 50 percent of pet owners would rather be stranded on a desert island with their pet than with a person. [Animal League]

Appendix 2: Pearl's Favorite Waffle Recipe

—Recipe courtesy of Dana Cutts (aka The Small Tree, aka the Small Chef, aka Pearl's grandma).

Ingredients:

- ½ c. warm water (100-110 degrees)
- 1 pkg. active/instant dry yeast (2½ tsp. yeast approx.)
- 1 tsp. sugar
- 1 tsp. regular table salt
- 2 c. organic warm milk (100-110 degrees)
- 2 c. organic all-purpose flour
  (or 1½ c. all-purpose flour + ½ c. whole wheat pastry flour)
- ½ c. (1 stick) unsalted organic butter, cut into cubes
- 2 tsp. white sesame seeds, flax seeds, millet seeds, other seed garnish as desired (optional)
- 2 large organic eggs
- ¼ tsp. baking soda (*Make sure soda is very fresh!*)

Instructions:
Put warm water in a drinking glass, sprinkle sugar and yeast over it, stir and cover it to "proof." Let mixture stand for several minutes until it looks dissolved and foamy.

Pour into a large mixing bowl (dough will rise to twice its volume).

Stir in salt, warm milk, butter, flour. Beat briskly with a spoon until smooth and blended.

Cover bowl with plastic wrap. Let stand overnight in a cool kitchen or in the fridge.

Just before cooking on your warmed-up waffle iron, beat in the eggs and any other desired garnish*. Then add in the baking soda.

Batter will be very thin and will keep for several days, covered, in the fridge—or you can make all the waffles at once and then freeze the rest. To reheat, just pop them in a toaster, toaster oven or regular oven.

---

* *Waffles should be served as a **treat only** because of the yeast, sugar, and salt. You can also remove the yeast, sugar, and/or salt as desired and add in flax seed, millet, quinoa, etc., to make your own waffle-flavored healthy "birdie bread."*

Thankfuls: *Pearl*

[NOTE: *In our flock, the family member with the feathers always gets to go first.*]

Pearl is very thankful for waffles.

He would like to thank every waffle in the world (those already eaten, those "en plate," and those not yet eaten) and let them know he loves them very much.

He also loves YOU—his VIP fans.

He loves his grandpa (aka the Tall Tree) and his grandma (aka the Small Tree, aka the Small Chef) so very much.

And he loves his mommy, who loves him to infinity and beyond.

Thankfuls: *Shannon*

I want to thank Pearl. Wherever you are, I will always be.

Many thanks to PetSmart for giving me the chance of a lifetime to meet my feathery soulmate.

Thanks to Cape Cod, the most inspiring possible place to bring a new book into the world.

A deep thank you from my heart to my wonderful agent and dear friend, Laurie Harper, who partnered with me on this project, helped me develop my vision, supported me to find just the right publishing approach and—most of all—encouraged me to "set Pearl free to work his magic on the world" (her beautiful words, not mine).

Thank you to my editor, Jaime Gjerdingen, for editing each one of Pearl's stories with such care.

Muchas gracias to the patient, talented team of behind-the-scenes graphics and publication whisperers who worked with me to craft such a perfect book cover, logo, and layout.

Infinite gratitude and love to my mom and dad, Dana and Paul Cutts, who cheered me on right from day one, listened intently to each draft chapter (sometimes many times), offered up thoughtful comments, pre-ordered zillions of copies, and lavished love (and plenty of waffles) on us both.

Special thanks to Mom, who fired up her Masters in Education to edit the first full draft! WOW.

To J.P. Morgan—you will always be with us through these pages.

With grateful thanks to my treasured volunteer advance readers who read and re-read various drafts and strengthened our story with your insights and inspiration.

Much love to my dear ones—you have mentored and supported me throughout, each in some essential way (you know who you are!).

Big grateful HUGS to Pearl's VIP fans—both feathered and featherless. Every day is better with feathers…and you.

Shannon

Author Bios

Shannon Cutts is first and foremost a birdie and tortoise mama. She is also a writer, speaker, nonprofit founder, mentor, lover of retro threads, and champion of all things (and beings) recovered and recovering. *Love & Feathers* is her second book.

Connect with Shannon: **shannoncutts.com**

Pearl Cutts is fetching and feathery. He is a Golden Waffle Award−winning actor best known for his role as .007, pint-sized superspy. He also serves as CEO/super(bird)model for *Wet Bird Couture*. Pearl loves waffles and ladybirds and his ever-expanding flock of VIP fans (both feathered and featherless).

Connect with Pearl: **loveandfeathers.com**

CPSIA information can be obtained
at www.ICGtesting.com
Printed in the USA
FSOW01n0106121115
13296FS